Poisonous Snakes of Texas

POISONOUS SNAKES
of TEXAS

Andrew H. Price

TEXAS PARKS *and* WILDLIFE PRESS

Publisher and Editor: Georg Zappler
Designer: Barbara M. Whitehead
Printing: Jolley Printing, Houston, Texas

ISBN: 1-885696-22-1

Texas Parks and Wildlife Department
4200 Smith School Road
Austin, Texas 78744

CONTENTS

PREFACE

This publication was first issued in 1950 in response to many requests for a condensed, illustrated guide to the venomous snakes of Texas. The fact that it was reprinted seven times, but has been out of print since 1978, and that the Texas Parks and Wildlife Department continues to receive requests for it, reflects the continuing interest in the subject. The book was initially written in response to the widespread fear and misinformation regarding snakes and snakebite in Texas. There is no doubt that a venomous snakebite can become a major medical emergency, and this book still serves the primary purpose of introducing the very latest knowledge concerning prevention and treatment. I have expanded that mission, however, and attempt also to introduce the reader to the ecological and evolutionary context in which these snakes live. My intention is to inform the interested reader about the myths and realities regarding the biological characteristics of Texas' venomous snakes. My desire is to lessen the hatred and fear and to increase the understanding of venomous snakes, the respect with which they are treated, and the appreciation with which they should be regarded.

Fifteen kinds of venomous snakes (species and subspecies) are found in Texas. Each kind is illustrated in this guide by a color photograph, and its distribution is shown by a range map. Unshaded counties on a given range map indicate the absence of a known specimen for that species. Accompanying text provides the common and scientific name, a general description, a comparison with similar species found in Texas and summary sketches of habitat, behavior, reproduction, diet and venom. With this information, the reader should have little difficulty learning to recognize the venomous snakes found in specific parts of the state.

The references listed in the bibliography have been used in the preparation of this revised publication. In addition, for those who wish to delve deeper into the biology of venomous snakes in particular or into the science of herpetology in general, I recommend the following sources: There are many local herpetology clubs, as well as regional groups (such as the Texas Herpetological Society), and three international societies based in the United States devoted to the study of amphibians and reptiles. They are: the American Society of Ichthyologists and Herpetologists (ASIH, founded in 1913 and publisher of the journal *Copeia*); the Herpetologists' League (HL, founded in 1936 and publisher of the journals *Herpetologica* and *Herpetological Monographs*); and the Society for the Study of Amphibians and Reptiles (SSAR, founded in 1967 and publisher of the *Journal of Herpetology, Herpetological Review* and *Catalogue of American Amphibians and Reptiles,* as well as a number of books and pamphlets). Readers interested in joining these organizations may call or write me for further information.

The photographs in this book are from the 1978 edition, except for those of the Southern Copperhead (photographed by Earl Nottingham) and the Banded Rock Rattlesnake (photographed by Carl S. Lieb). Most of the line drawings are also from the 1978 edition. Some additional drawings, showing pitviper behaviors, were prepared by Barbara Whitehead.

I am indebted to John E. Werler, the author of the previous editions of this book, for the many years he devoted to educating the people of Texas about their natural heritage. I am grateful to Georg Zappler and Matt Wagner of the Texas Parks and Wildlife Department for patiently and persistently encouraging me to write the revised version of this book, and also for their editorial reviews. I thank Alan Keller and Brian King of the Statistical Services Division, Bureau of Vital Statistics, Texas Department of Health, for providing me with the updated figures on selected sources of mortality in Texas. I extend my appreciation to Drs. Jonathan A. Campbell (University of Texas at Arlington), Don Connell, M.D. (Austin, Texas), Richard C. Dart, M.D. (Rocky Mountain Poison and Drug Center, Denver, Colorado), James R. Dixon (Texas A&M University), Frederick R. Gehlbach (Baylor University), Harry W. Greene (University of California, Berkeley), David L. Hardy, M.D. (Tucson, Arizona), Jerry D. Johnson (El Paso Community College), William W. Lamar (Tyler, Texas) and Sherman A. Minton, M.D. (Indianapolis, Indiana) for reviewing all or parts of this book. These colleagues significantly improved the clarity of the manuscript; any remaining errors are my own. Finally, I thank my wife Barbara for reading the manuscript from a layperson's point of view and providing me with her input, and for tolerating my fascination with the subjects of this book.

Andrew H. Price, Ph. D.
Conservation Scientist
Texas Parks and Wildlife Department
4200 Smith School Road
Austin, Texas 78744
(512) 912-7022
email: andy.price@tpwd.state.tx.us

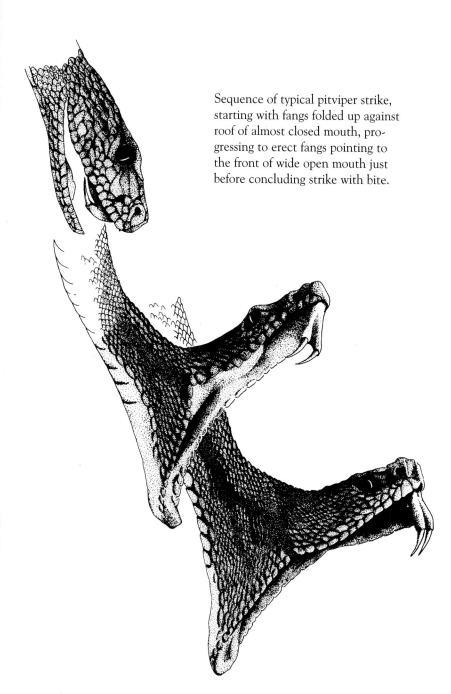

Sequence of typical pitviper strike, starting with fangs folded up against roof of almost closed mouth, progressing to erect fangs pointing to the front of wide open mouth just before concluding strike with bite.

INTRODUCTION

The fact that snakes and lizards are closely related is reflected by the placement of the two groups within the same taxonomic category—the reptilian order Squamata. The precise origin of snakes, however, remains uncertain. Snakes and lizards could have evolved as separate lineages of an ancient group, the Lepidosauria, or they could have evolved from a common lepidosaurian ancestor. It is most likely that snakes actually evolved from lizards, the earliest representatives of which are known from the fossil record to have existed some 230 million years ago during the Paleozoic/Mesozoic transition. The earliest unambiguous snake fossil appeared in the early Cretaceous, about 135 million years ago. Diversification of the snake group had occurred by the late Cretaceous/Paleocene transition (70–65 million years ago), and by the Miocene (22.5 million years ago) the dominant modern families, Colubridae, Elapidae and Viperidae, were present. Most biologists believe that snake ancestors were adapted to a secretive or semi-burrowing existence, since their descendants possess a number of characteristics suggestive of such an existence—namely, body elongation, modification of internal organs (including extreme elongation and/or loss of paired structure), loss of limbs and extreme reduction or loss of supporting shoulder and hip girdles, replacement of movable eyelids with a transparent cap over the eye, rearrangement and increased complexity of jaw and head muscles, and complete separation of the right and left halves of the lower jaw so that each half can be moved independently. Some recent fossil evidence suggests that the lizard ancestors of snakes may have been aquatic forms, probably related to the mosasaurs—a group of giant marine lizards that became extinct at the same time as the dinosaurs. Indeed, many of the features listed above could just as readily be aquatic adaptations. Whatever the original line of descent, the ability to capture prey through constriction and the use of venom were later developments. Today snakes, along with lizards, are the most numerous reptiles on earth; they can be found on all continents except Antarctica and they inhabit many oceans.

Despite the ready availability of information about almost any subject, venomous snakes and snakebite remain mysterious to most people. More than one recent survey has revealed that people are more afraid of snakes than they are of almost any other group of organisms; this probably reflects a relationship extending far back into human prehistory. Given the abundance and diversity of snakes in Texas and the increasing frequency with which Texans and visitors from elsewhere are exploring the outdoors, it is essential that accurate knowledge be available about the identification, distribution and biological characteristics of the state's venomous reptiles, as well as about the relative risks of snakebite, how to prevent it, and how to treat it should it occur.

The first major study of the incidence of venomous snakebite in Texas was reported in 1927 by Afranio do Amaral, then director of the Antivenom Institute of America. During the twelve-month period from July 1926 to June 1927, a total of 150 cases of snakebite envenomation (venom injection) were known to have occurred in

Texas, 28 of them fatal. A subsequent survey by R. H. Hutchison showed that 163 cases of snakebite were reported in 1928, 9 of which resulted in death. John Werler of the Houston Zoo recorded 1,318 snakebites in Texas during the five-year period from 1949 to 1953; 18 of these were fatal.

Henry M. Parrish reported on 559 snakebite cases seen by Texas physicians in 1958 and 1959. Sufficient information was available about 461 of these cases to extract information. Rattlesnakes were involved in 47% of the 461 cases, copperheads were involved in 22%, cottonmouths in 7% and coral snakes in 1%; a full 23% of the cases involved unidentified venomous snakes. Bites were less frequent (or perhaps just less frequently reported) in the sparsely populated western third of the state, and were particularly high around larger cities (Austin, Beaumont, El Paso, Dallas/Fort Worth, Houston, Port Arthur and San Antonio). Ninety-seven percent of all snakebites reported in the survey occurred between April and November, when snakes are most active and when people are more likely to be outdoors. The largest proportion of bite victims (46%) were under 20 years of age, highlighting the importance of supervising young children closely when they are in areas where venomous snakes are known to occur, and of instructing older children and teenagers in matters of snakebite prevention.

Most recently, T. G. Glass reported on 175 snakebite cases he personally treated in the San Antonio area from 1966 to 1975. The victims ranged in age from 18 months to 85 years, with more than twice as many males as females being bitten (121 versus 54). The snakes inflicting the bites were Western Diamondback Rattlesnakes (*Crotalus atrox;* 135, or 77%), Copperheads (*Agkistrodon contortrix;* 30, or 17%), Cottonmouths (*Agkistrodon piscivorus;* 5, or 3%) and Coral Snakes (*Micrurus fulvius;* 5, or 3%). Of those, 101 bites (75%) from Western Diamondbacks, 19 bites (63%) from Copperheads and 3 bites (60%) from Cottonmouths were treated surgically on the basis of the appearance of local symptoms such as swelling or tenderness. This level of surgical intervention is considered unnecessary by most medical personnel today. The removal of dead or infected tissue revealed obvious signs of intramuscular injection of venom in 69 (56%) of the cases. Bites occurred most often on the leg (33%), 28% of bites were on the foot or ankle, 20% were on the finger, and 15% were on the hand or arm. Fourteen patients developed blood-clotting problems, 16 were treated with antivenom, 13 developed serum sickness, and one 85-year-old woman died from complete defibrination (see glossary) of the plasma and a cerebral hemorrhage.

In general surveys of more than 1,300 snakebite cases from southern states during the 1960s and 1970s by L. H. S. Van Mierop and Henry Parrish and colleagues, 25% of the cases were "dry bites," meaning that fang marks were present, but there was little if any pain because little or no venom was injected, and no medical treatment was necessary. Mild envenomation with slight swelling and pain occurred in 39% of the cases, and required minimal medical treatment and usually no administration of antivenom. Moderate envenomation accompanied by pain, swelling, nausea and other symptoms of shock occurred in 22% of the cases, and required medical attention and the administration of antivenom. Finally, severe envenomation with heightened symptoms, including unconsciousness in some cases, occurred in 14% of the cases, which required hospitalization and treatment with high levels of antivenom.

Snakebites are relatively rare compared with accidents resulting from other outdoor-related activities, as shown by comparative data from the Bureau of Vital Statistics, Texas Department of Health (see p. 10). One aim of the 1978 edition of this book was to reduce the incidence of snakebite by educating people about the nature of venomous snakes and how to be better prepared to deal with such a contingency during outdoor activities. The subsequent threefold reduction in the yearly average rate of death from snakebite in Texas (2.7 versus 1.0), especially when compared with increases in death rates from automobiles (3,511 versus 3,698), boating accidents (57 versus 67) and firearm accidents (10 versus 171), may be attributed to the success of such educational efforts as well as to advances in medical treatment. Again, however, I urge every Texan to obtain a thorough working knowledge of the correct first-aid treatment for snakebite, so that proper action may be taken should it become necessary. Preventing a bite from happening is at least as important, and a necessary step toward attaining this goal is gathering knowledge about the habits, distribution and behavior of venomous snakes and how to identify such snakes. A further step is to understand the evolutionary adaptations of venomous snakes and their behavior patterns and, in a larger sense, to reintegrate humankind with the natural world. This book is intended as a small contribution toward meeting that goal.

Annual human deaths from selected outdoor activities in Texas, 1978-1996

Year	Auto	Drowning	Nondrown Boating	Firearm Hunting	Lightning	Venomous Arthopod	Snakebite
1978	4,140	510	93	196	11	5	1
1979	3,981	495	86	164	5	6	2
1980	4,295	494	86	199	5	2	1
1981	4,580	452	70	222	4	5	1
1982	4,199	472	78	250	13	2	2
1983	3,899	500	93	200	5	5	0
1984	4,030	375	61	203	5	5	0
1985	3,824	443	70	218	6	4	1
1986	3,712	436	60	172	6	3	3
1987	3,315	396	63	141	2	5	1
1988	3,460	359	62	154	9	3	0
1989	3,476	337	62	172	2	3	2
1990	3,309	327	53	171	6	3	1
1991	3,180	340	50	179	6	8	0
1992	3,147	352	62	174	3	2	0
1993	3,184	344	57	156	4	2	0
1994	3,307	281	60	116	9	6	0
1995	3,302	310	54	84	6	8	2
1996	3,925	281	51	77	5	6	2

Precautions at Home

Statistics show that a large percentage of bites occur near the home. Although a few of these are inflicted upon small children playing in their own backyards, many are what physicians refer to as "illegitimate bites," resulting from people taking unnecessary or foolish risks with venomous snakes. Every year zoos, animal control officers and other wildlife agency personnel receive calls from distressed homeowners who have discovered rattlesnakes or copperheads beneath their house, in the garage or under trash piles. They ask for assistance in removing the snake and preventing a recurrence. Unfortunately, such incidents will only become more frequent as human populations grow, cities expand into snake habitats and greater numbers of people want to live closer to "natural" or "pristine" areas. Venomous snakes are a fact of life in Texas; encounters can be managed and minimized but not eliminated. Unfortunately, none of the commercially available "snake-proofing" devices, chemical or mechanical, have ever been demonstrated to be completely reliable.

Snakes, including the venomous kinds, occur around a home for two reasons: food and shelter. Snakes are found in or underneath objects either because those objects also attract their prey, such as rodents, or because the snakes are escaping inhospitable weather conditions. The attractions of a dwelling to a venomous snake can be minimized by moving the objects that attract rodents and other prey items, such as trash dumps, brush and woodpiles, and by constructing barns and livestock sheds as far away as possible from your home. Anticipate that overturned boats, trailers, tarps and similar objects may provide temporary shelter for a snake moving through the area. Snakes are adept at getting through seemingly impenetrable tiny openings, and this should be kept in mind when attempting to close off a base-ment, a detached garage, or a shed. Keep such areas as neat and tidy as possible, and remember that snakes seek out such areas for peace and quiet and so are likely to be tucked away somewhere instead of being obvious in the middle of the floor.

Charles M. Bogert, late curator of herpetology at the American Museum of Natural History, once suggested the use of a quarter-inch-mesh wire fence to keep snakes off res-idential property. This yard-high snakeproof fence is placed around the house in much the same manner as an ordinary picket fence, except that the bottom must be set about six inches down into the ground to prevent snakes from forcing their way beneath it. In addition, all gates must be provided with close-fitting sills on the bottoms and sides to ensure a completely tight enclosure. Experiments were done on fences of this kind to determine their effectiveness and to seek possible improvements in their construction. Copperheads and small rattlesnakes could not get over the vertically straight fence, but a six-foot rattlesnake used in the experiment was able to climb over, with the result that one important change was made: When the same fence was tilted outward at a 30-degree angle, not even the largest snake was able to reach the top. Although such fences are expensive and difficult to keep in good repair, they may be desirable under extreme circumstances. Electrical fences have been tried in certain situations, such as the invasion of the Pacific island of Guam by the Brown Tree Snake (*Boiga irregularis*), with some success. These fences are at least 2 feet (60 cm) high, with vegetation cleared away an equal distance from both sides. They are usually constructed of vinyl netting or similar material and are most effective if several electrical strands are embedded in each fence.

Protection in the Field

Venomous snakes are more common in rural areas, where they present a greater hazard to human life than elsewhere. Consequently farmers, ranchers, hunters and fishermen, hikers and campers, and others who spend a great deal of time outdoors should take extra care in avoiding a bite. Because most snakebites are inflicted on the arms or legs, they require special protection. The use of a little caution when placing hands and feet where snakes may be partially or completely hidden from view is the best protection. This is particularly true when climbing on rocky ledges where your hands may reach the level of the ledge before your eyes do. In some parts of the state rattlesnakes and copperheads are common on such rocky hillsides where, especially during the warm days of early spring or late fall, they coil and sun themselves.

Packrat middens and armadillo burrows also make excellent shelters for rattlesnakes, and it is foolhardy to reach into one of these holes. Yet, during one year in South Texas alone, two people are known to have been bitten by rattlesnakes when they reached into armadillo holes searching for small game animals.

Another way to invite snakebite is to turn over a log or similar object thoughtlessly with bare hands or to step over one without first looking to see if a snake is coiled on the other side. Many snakes, particularly copperheads and coral snakes, often hide beneath or within decaying logs, and such habitats should be considered a potential snake haven. If a log must be moved, use a long stick or garden tool. Stepping over a log will be less risky if boots or high-top shoes are worn, but even then it is safer first to check to see what may be on the other side.

Several types of footwear offer good protection against the bites of most snakes: high-top leather shoes, riding boots, rubber boots or a combination of army "paratrooper shoes" and heavy leather puttees are particularly good. For protection of the legs above the knees, snakeproof trousers that weigh little more than those of ordinary duck material are available. They consist of three thicknesses of duck material and one layer of fine wire mesh, flexible enough to allow easy knee movement. Snakeproof leggings of a similar material can be purchased for safeguarding just the lower legs. Aluminum or plastic leggings furnish good protection in many cases, but some brands may be thin and easily damaged, while some others are simply uncomfortable.

If a venomous snake is discovered active nearby, the best reaction is to remain as still as possible until the snake has moved away. It should be remembered that a snake may be quick to strike at a moving object, so to step away at such a moment may stimulate the snake to strike. If a rattlesnake is heard nearby but cannot be located, do not begin a wild dash for safety. The location of the snake may be misjudged and by taking a step you may walk into rather than away from it. Again, remain still until the snake is sighted. When it is certain the reptile is at least five or six feet distant and is the only snake in the vicinity, slowly back away. If you must move away before locating the snake, do so as slowly as possible.

Our native venomous snakes are mostly nocturnal in their activities, usually remaining hidden during the day and emerging at night in search of food. Because of this, you should use a flashlight if it is necessary to travel on foot through snake country after dark. This is true even around your home, particularly if you live in newly expanding suburbs or in rural areas. During the cooler days of spring and autumn, however, these daily habits of snakes are often reversed; during the day they will be searching for warm spots in which to sun themselves, and by nightfall they are again under cover.

Ordinarily, no type of venomous snake found in Texas can strike farther than a distance equal to three-quarters of its body length unless it is supported by firm ground or is striking downward on an incline. Certainly, none has the ability to jump at a target, a feat often erroneously attributed to rattlesnakes. A snake on the defensive is coiled with the forward part of the body in a loose "S" position. When the snake is striking, this coil is straightened out and the head is thrust forward. It is not necessary for a snake to strike from a coil in order to bite; if picked up, it may simply turn and bite the hand that is holding it.

Recognizing the Venomous Kinds of Snakes

The ability to differentiate harmless snakes from venomous ones is an important component to managing the risk and treatment of snakebite. Only fifteen of the approximately 120 different kinds of snakes native to Texas are dangerous to humans, and some of these are so infrequently encountered that they are not much of a threat. In addition to these, there are several species of smaller snakes in Texas known as *opisthoglyphs* ("rear-fanged"), which possess a relatively mild venom and a set of small, grooved fangs set far back on the upper jaw. They are considered harmless to humans because of their unaggressive behavior, weak and limited supply of venom, and small fangs which are poorly adapted for injecting venom into large animals. Most of these, including the black-headed snakes (genus *Tantilla*) which are found throughout the state, are less than 15" (380 mm) long and thinner than a pencil. The slightly larger Night Snake (*Hypsiglena torquata*) of west and central Texas has enlarged but ungrooved teeth in the upper jaw. Two Mexican species found as far north as the King Ranch (Norias Division) are somewhat larger: the Black-Striped Snake *(Coniophanes imperialis)* reaches about 20" (500 mm) in length and the Cat-Eyed Snake *(Leptodeira septentrionalis)* is up to 36" (900 mm) long. Another rarely seen species is the Lyre Snake *(Trimorphodon biscutatus)*, found in extreme west Texas.

In spite of the small number of venomous kinds of snakes in Texas, no one general rule can be used to safely identify all of them at a glance. It is, for example, a mistaken idea that all venomous snakes have broad, triangular heads; in fact, if one uses this rule, many of our harmless snakes look more dangerous than the venomous ones. Hognose snakes (genus *Heterodon*), water snakes (genus *Nerodia*) and garter snakes (genus *Thamnophis*)—all of which are non-venomous— can all flatten their heads by laterally expanding their jaw muscles as part of their defensive display, whereas the highly venomous Texas Coral Snake has a small, narrow head. The characteristic rattle of a rattlesnake may be missing under certain unusual circumstances, rendering its identification more difficult. Rattlesnakes frequently do not rattle before initially striking, so don't expect a warning—it might not come. Also, a rattlesnake may frequently be coiled in such a way that the rattle is hidden beneath the snake's body, and therefore the snake must be recognized by different means.

Disregard all of the so-called easy rules by which venomous snakes can be identified, and instead learn to know each one by the combination of its most characteristic features. For example, to identify the Cottonmouth, look for a relatively short, stout body and a broad, flat head. Do not try to look for the light color of the inside of the mouth. However, **do** look for a body color of black, dark brown or olive and a pattern of 10–15 wide, usually indistinct crossbands which are generally lighter in the center than on the edges. Additionally, the upper jaw below the eye and the lower jaw will be light colored in contrast to the dark color of the remainder of the head. Together, these characteristics will make identification quite certain from a reasonable distance. Remember that the young of this species are colored differently from the adults and that you may not be able to identify the juveniles from the same characteristics that you use to identify the adults.

An additional complicating factor in identification occurs when a snake's markings are temporarily obscured, making recognition more difficult. Approximately ten days before snakes shed their skins, the eyes and color pattern appear milky and opaque (the "blue" phase), but clear again a few days before they shed. During this period when the snake's pattern and colors are dulled, identification may not be easy. Incidentally, venomous snakes are generally more irritable at this time and may be more prone to strike then, since they are essentially blind and may be physiologically stressed. Consider also that snakes with abnormal features of color and pattern sometimes occur among populations of normal-looking individuals; there may be all-white specimens, all-yellow ones or those that are completely black. Such aberrant individuals are rare; even so, the more you familiarize yourself with the normal colors, markings and overall appearance of a species, the easier it will be to recognize the occasional abnormally pigmented specimen.

Venom

Snake venoms are complex substances, containing a large number of proteins with multiple lethal enzyme fractions, the specific composition of which varies among species and sometimes from one individual to another within a species (see, for example, the accounts for the Timber Rattlesnake and the Mojave Rattlesnake). The importance of understanding the effects of specific enzyme components of venom and of being able to identify the venomous species which occur naturally in Texas cannot be overemphasized in terms of its significance in the management and treatment of snakebite. Among lethal venom components are the following:

• **neurotoxins,** which interfere with chemical communication between nerve cells (and thus nerve function), or between nerves (including those responsible for regulating breathing) and muscle cells at neuromuscular junctions; when these are involved, death usually results from asphyxiation;

• **proteolytic enzymes,** which destroy blood plasma proteins such as those involved in blood clotting, as well as collagen and other elastic connective tissues, resulting in the digestion and consequent damage of local tissue;

• **myonecrotic enzymes,** which specifically destroy the functional microanatomy of muscles, perhaps through massive disruption of the ability of the membrane enclosing muscle fibers to regulate influx of Na^+ (sodium ions) and through disruption of ion-regulation functions in general;

• **hemorrhagic and hemolytic enzymes,** the first of which causes blood to leak through vessel walls, while the latter destroys red blood cells; both cause a reduction in blood pressure and disrupt the delivery of oxygen to tissues;

• **cardiovascular enzymes,** which specifically attack heart muscle, decreasing cardiac output and perturbing blood pressure ratios;

• **cytolytic enzymes,** which disrupt cellular function and destroy other cells in the body.

Several major enzyme constituents of snake venom, such as phospholipase A_2, may be present in multiple isoforms (see glossary) in a particular species or individual snake, each isoform contributing to one of the major lethal effects outlined above.

Individual snakes possess a limited quantity of venom at any one time, and what they have is "expensive" to make in terms of the metabolic resources required. This may help explain why little or no venom is injected in 20%–40% of human venomous snakebite cases (so-called dry bites) in Texas; venom is a precious commodity as the primary means whereby a snake obtains a meal, and it is not going to waste it on anything else unless absolutely necessary. In those cases in which venom is injected, the yield and toxicity depend upon a number of variables; for the snake, these include the time interval since it last expended venom (which can take up to four days to resynthesize), the snake's age, size and general health, environmental and seasonal effects, geographic location, and individual variation (genetic effects). Many of these factors are also important in victims in determining the outcome of a venomous snakebite. A snakebite is likely to be more serious for the very young or very old, or for someone whose physiology is already compromised by disease or illness. In addition, the location of the bite on the body is important; bites on the extremities are less life-threatening and more easily treated than those closer to or on the trunk. The most important factor in the seriousness of a venomous snakebite, however, is the timeliness and quality of medical care provided to the victim.

The strength of a given snake species' venom, or the "lethal dosage," is usually expressed as an LD_{50} value. This is the venom dosage, expressed as milligrams of venom per kilogram of the test animal (mice are usually used), which will kill 50% of the experimental subjects during a 24-hour period in a clinical trial.

The following table illustrates the variation discussed above.

Percentage of snakebite victims exhibiting a variety of symptoms from rattlesnake bites (from Russell, 1983)

Fang marks / 100
Swelling and edema / 74
Pain / 65
Ecchymosis* / 51
Vesiculations* / 40
Changes in pulse rate / 60
Weakness / 72
Sweating and/or chills / 64
Numbness or tingling of tongue and mouth, or scalp
    or feet / 63
Faintness or dizziness / 57
Nausea, vomiting, or both / 48
Blood pressure changes / 46
Change in body temperature / 31
Swelling of regional lymph nodes / 40
Fasciculations* / 41
Increased blood-clotting time / 39
Sphering of red blood cells / 18
Tingling or numbness of affected part / 42
Necrosis* / 27
Respiratory rate changes / 40
Decreased hemoglobin / 37
Abnormal electrocardiogram / 26
Cyanosis* / 16
Hematemesis,* hematuria,* or melena* / 15
Glycosuria* / 20
Proteinuria* / 16
Unconsciousness / 12
Thirst / 34
Increased salivation / 20
Swollen eyelids / 2
Retinal hemorrhage / 2
Blurring of vision / 12
Convulsions / 1
Muscle contractions / 6
Increased blood platelets / 4
Decreased blood platelets / 42

* See glossary

Snakebite

Texas' snakes, including the venomous ones, are success-ful components of the natural ecosystems to which they belong; their ability to remain inconspicuous to potential enemies, including humans, is an element of this success. Sensing danger, a snake which is alert is more likely to move off without first being detected by the average person out-doors. Failing that, a snake is most likely to remain hidden or stationary, and to rely upon camouflage or threatening behavior, such as striking with a closed mouth, vibrating its tail, flattening and/or inflating its body, and hissing, or, in the case of rattlesnakes, rattling. It is only from an acute sense of danger that a snake is likely to bite. On the other hand, any snake is likely to bite if startled or surprised by, for example, being stepped on while asleep; in such cases, rat-tlesnakes are likely to bite without rattling first. Although snakebite is an unlikely event, it makes sense to have a con-tingency plan. Prior planning can be the most important contribution to surviving a venomous snakebite.

Precautions

These include:
1. Learn to recognize the snakes that are likely to occur in the area in which you are or will be. This is important should treatment be necessary, and may prevent the killing of harm-less snakes.

2. Minimize the chances of an unfortunate encounter with a venomous snake by learning about snakes' habits, when and where they are likely to be active and under what conditions they are likely to strike.

3. Be sensible. Don't walk around after dark in snake

country collecting firewood or engaging in other activities without a light. Don't put your hands or feet in places which might conceal a snake without checking first. Don't sit down on the ground without inspecting the surrounding area. Don't crawl beneath fences without first looking underneath them carefully. Don't sleep near wood or rubbish piles, at the entrance to a cave or near swampy areas.

4. Be careful. Dress appropriately, wearing suitable boots or shoes and long pants or other protective clothing where encounters are likely to occur. A normal defensive strike by a pitviper at ground level is unlikely to penetrate boots or canvas pants, and a number of "snakeproof" leggings are commercially available.

5. Be smart. Don't play around with live or dead venomous snakes; some snakes thought to have been dead have been known to bite and inject venom. Physicians emphasize the fact that approximately half of the bites treated annually are "illegitimate"; that is, they result from interactions with snakes which are deliberately brought about by the person who ends up being bitten.

6. Be prepared. Know what to do (and what **not** to do) when engaging in activities in which encounters with venomous snakes are a possibility.

First Aid

Recommended measures are:
1. Assume envenomation has occurred, especially if initial symptoms are present. Initial symptoms from pitviper bites include fang puncture marks (see opposite page); in addition, they almost always include immediate burning pain at the bite site, immediate and usually progressive local swelling within five minutes, as well as local discoloration of the skin (*ecchymosis—*

Bite Pattern (*Modified from Pope and Perkins, 1944*)

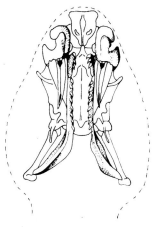

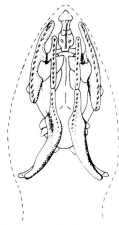

Upper jaw of pit viper viewed from below, showing the two fangs and two parallel rows of smaller teeth between them.

Upper jaw of bullsnake (nonvenomous) viewed from below, showing the four rows of small teeth.

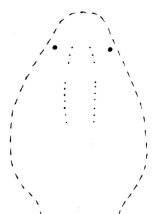

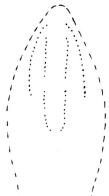

Typical pitviper bite pattern. Note two large fang punctures (smaller rows of tooth punctures may or may not be present).

Typical nonvenomous snakebite pattern. Note *absence* of two large fang punctures (incomplete bites occasionally result in omission of part of pattern).

see glossary) due to the destruction of blood vessels and red blood cells. Initial symptoms from coral-snake bites include tremors, slurred speech, blurred or double vision, drowsiness or euphoria and a marked increase in salivation within four hours; however, life-threatening effects from coral snake envenomation may not be evident for 24 hours or longer.

2. Identify the species of venomous snake that inflicted the bite. This may provide useful information for emergency medical personnel attempting to judge the onset and severity of symptoms, although identification is not necessary to ensure proper clinical treatment. Appropriate precautions should be taken in attempting to identify the snake, so as to avoid having another person bitten.

3. Keep the victim as calm as possible. This helps reduce the spread of venom and the onset of shock to an already stressed physiological system.

4. Keep yourself and any other members of the group calm as well. This will help reassure the victim and ensure that the appropriate first-aid measures are followed, as well as preventing anyone else from becoming injured.

5. Know and be alert for the symptoms of shock, and institute the proper treatment should it ensue. Difficulty in breathing and/or kidney failure are frequent symptoms of envenomation.

6. Wash the bite area with a disinfectant if available.

7. Remove jewelry such as rings and watches, as well as tight-fitting clothes, before the onset of swelling.

8. Reduce or prevent movement of a bitten extremity, using a splint if possible; this helps decrease the spread of venom. For the same reason, position the extremity below the level of the heart.

9. Get the victim to a medical facility as soon as possible and begin treatment there with intravenous antivenom, crystalloid solutions and antibiotics. Antivenom treatment is generally most effective within the first four hours of envenomation, and is ineffective after 8–10 hours.

The following should be avoided:

1. Do not make incisions over the bite marks. This can result in significant damage to already traumatized tissue, and can damage intact structures such as nerves and blood vessels, enhance bleeding caused by anticoagulant components of venom and increase the rapid spread of venom throughout the body if the circulatory system is compromised. A suction device, such as the Sawyer *Extractor*^{TM}, may be used without making any incisions. This device may remove significant quantities of venom, although its efficacy has yet to be conclusively determined.

2. Do not use a tourniquet or other constricting band except in extreme cases of envenomation, and then only if properly trained in the technique. Such devices are of no value if applied more than thirty minutes after the bite, and if improperly used they can restrict vital blood flow to the traumatized tissue and possibly result in the amputation of an extremity. Unbearable pain can also result, and the improper loosening of such devices can allow sudden systemic absorption of venom.

3. Do not use cryotherapy (including cold compresses, ice, dry ice, chemical ice packs, spray refrigerants, and freezing) for the same reasons that tourniquets should be avoided, and also because it can increase the area of necrosis.

4. Do not use electroshock therapy, a method popularized following publication of a letter from a missionary in South America reporting its effectiveness in treating bites from snakes of uncertain identity. Several controlled clinical trials and at least one on humans have failed to demonstrate any positive result; moreover, the potential negative results from the uncontrolled use of an electric charge are obvious.

5. Do not drink alcohol, as it dilates blood vessels and increases absorption from the circulatory system, and thus helps spread venom faster.

6. Do not use aspirin or related medications to relieve pain, because they increase bleeding. A pain reliever not containing aspirin, however, may be used.

7. Do not use the pressure/immobilization technique, which consists of firmly wrapping the entire limb with an elastic bandage and then splinting, especially for pitviper bites. The theory behind this treatment is to confine the venom to the area of the bite until reaching a medical facility, but studies have shown the technique to be ineffective or worse with venoms which produce local swelling and tissue damage.

8. Do not administer antivenom in the field unless properly trained in the procedure, unless evacuation to a medical facility will take many hours or days, or unless envenomation has been extreme. Intramuscular or subcutaneous application of antivenom has proven to be much less effective, and in some cases ineffective, than intravenous administration. Acute allergic reactions to antivenom can occur, and contemplated field administration of antivenom should include provision for a sufficient supply of epinephrine (adrenalin) to counteract any such potential effects.

Medical Treatment:

Providing long-term care and aiding recovery, the details of which will vary somewhat in each case, are best left to the discretion of trained and experienced medical personnel. Patients may take several weeks to recover from severe envenomations and symptoms may appear or recur anytime during this period, especially in cases where antivenom therapy is contraindicated, such as in patients who are allergic to such treatments. The prognosis is generally good in cases of muscle or tissue damage, providing that blood circulation and nerve connections to the affected area remain good and infection doesn't set in. Surgery is generally not called for except to relieve intramuscular compartmental pressure from swelling. Antivenom therapy can be greatly enhanced through the use of specific enzyme immunoassays on the patient's blood and other body fluids. Secondary complications, such as kidney failure, hypotension or anaphylaxis, are common and must be anticipated in treatment.

Antivenom therapy is only one component of successful treatment of envenomation by coral snakes. Patients should be observed for at least twenty-four hours, because paralysis from bites may not occur immediately. In cases of severe paralysis only an endotracheal intubation with mechanical ventilation will save the patient, as administration of antivenom will not reverse paralysis. Pneumonia, brain damage or death may result if ventilation is not performed quickly and appropriately; with proper ventilation the neuro-muscular blockade will gradually decrease and the patient will ultimately return to normal.

A final word is necessary for medical personnel. An "underground zoo" full of exotic venomous snakes kept by private individuals exists in Texas; hence, there is a need to identify the species involved in snakebite cases.

THE PITVIPERS

E xcept for one, all of the dangerously venomous snakes native to Texas are pitvipers—members of the subfamily Crotalinae (family Viperidae), although they are sometimes considered to belong to their own family, the Crotalidae. Roughly 160 pitviper species are distributed widely throughout temperate and tropical Asia and North and South America. They share with the true vipers the unique rotating, hinged-fang venom-delivery system called *solenoglyphy*. Briefly, here is how it works: The maxillae, the major tooth-bearing bones on either side of the upper jaw, are short and stout and bear no teeth other than the fangs. These are located on the front ends of the maxillae and are connected by ducts to the venom glands. Fangs are hollow, with an elongate opening on their front face; they are folded against the upper jaw along the roof of the mouth when not in use. Several skull bones are connected in a lever-and-pulley arrangement (see opposite), allowing each fang to pivot independently forward and downward, reaching an angle of 90° perpendicular to the jaw during a strike. A reserve fang series also exists, so that when a fang breaks or is shed, it is quickly replaced. There are two major venom glands—one on each side of the head behind the eye and above the angle of the jaw. An accessory gland of unknown function is situated along the outer edge of the upper jaw just below and forward of each eye. The main glands are surrounded by mus-

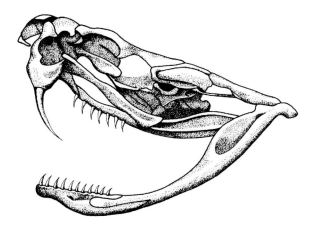

Skull of pitviper—side view showing the long, movable fang.

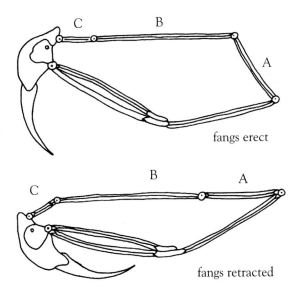

fangs erect

fangs retracted

Diagram of the poison apparatus of pitvipers showing the lever-and-pulley arrangement of the skull bones. *(from Klauber, 1972)*

cles which contract to expel venom. These muscles are separate from biting muscles, so snakes can control whether venom is injected, and if it is, how much. This series of adaptive characteristics allows vipers to take much heavier and bulkier prey than other venomous snakes, lessens the risks of harm from such prey to the individual snake, and has allowed the evolution of a stout, robust body form to occur.

Pitvipers are distinguished from other vipers by having specialized nerves, bearing receptors that are sensitive to infrared radiation. These infrared sensors are gathered together in one structure, the opening of which is located on each side of the face, between the eye and the nostril; it is this "pit" structure that gives the group as a whole its popular name. The receptors inside the pits pick up infrared radiation given off as body heat by a small prey animal, such as a rodent, and transmit this information to the snake's brain. There, an image is formed which overlaps with, and in some cases may be sharper than, that formed by the visual system. Infrared receptors are instrumental in guiding a pitviper's predatory strike. Boas and pythons also have heat sensors, but these are not gathered into a single structure; rather, they are dispersed along the upper and lower edges of the mouth.

All snakes use their tongue as a chemical identification system; thus, when a snake flicks out its tongue, it is in a sense "smelling" its environment. Odor molecules collect on the moist surface of the tongue and, when the snake retracts the tongue, these molecules are transferred to fleshy pads on the floor of the mouth. These pads in turn are pressed up against two small holes in the front part of the roof of the mouth, which lead to a unique structure called the Jacobson's Organ or, more generally, the vomeronasal organ (VNO). The VNO develops embryonically as an outpocketing of the nasal capsule, but becomes separated from it during development. The VNO is richly supplied with nerves which transmit chemical information to the brain.

This sensory system is very precise, allowing snakes to discriminate the sexual identity and receptivity of others of their kind during the mating season, as well as to identify enemies and prey. The forked structure of the tongue provides individual snakes with built-in feedback for following a chemical trail. As long as the stimulus intensity from both forks is approximately equal, the snake knows it is on the trail; if one side becomes stronger than the other, the snake can correct its direction until the signals are equal again. The VNO is a vital component of the feeding behavior of venomous snakes, such as pitvipers, that release their prey after striking. It provides a snake with the unique chemical "signature" of its prey, and allows the snake to find it, even though it may have traveled several meters before its death.

Pitvipers have many natural enemies despite their venomous nature. Some of these have developed a greater or lesser degree of immunity to pitviper venom, conferred by serum blood factors. Pitvipers in turn have evolved a most interesting defensive response when attacked by enemies immune to their venom, such as skunks or kingsnakes. Rather than exhibiting the classic coiled body with head

Pitviper driving off an attacker by using a clubbing motion. *(from Carpenter and Gillingham, 1975)*

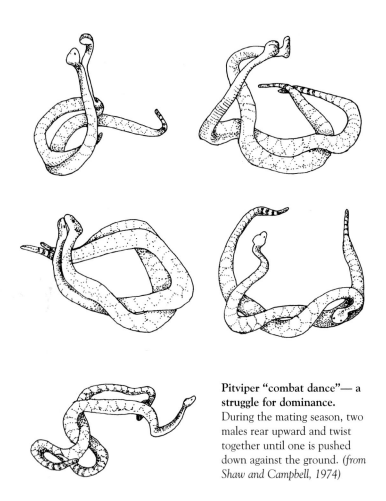

Pitviper "combat dance"— a struggle for dominance.
During the mating season, two males rear upward and twist together until one is pushed down against the ground. *(from Shaw and Campbell, 1974)*

poised to strike, pitvipers will position their bodies between the attacker and their own head and tail. Then, one or more loops of the body are raised in the air and brought down in a clubbing motion directed at the attacker in an attempt to drive it off. This peculiar behavior is elicited by specific chemical signals which the attackers possess and which pitvipers recognize through the VNO system described earlier.

Mating in pitvipers most often takes place in the spring,

but may also occur during the summer and fall. A male actively courts a female by slowly approaching her and rubbing his chin along her back, along with other precise body movements. Mating season is also the time when snake "dancing" is observed. These "dances" almost always involve two males twisting together and raising the front half of their bodies off the ground. The males are engaged in a struggle for dominance regardless of whether a female is actually nearby (see opposite).

All of the pitvipers that occur in Texas give birth to live young. A placenta-like structure is formed between the mother and the developing fetuses, and some degree of nutritional and waste exchange occurs across it. The young are born contained within a clear embryonic membrane from which they emerge within a minute or two after birth. All pitvipers in Texas can be distinguished from other snakes by the combination of the facial pit openings, vertically elliptical pupils, and a single row of scales—called subcaudal scales—on the underside of the tail.

Typical Pitviper Head
Side view showing facial pit and elliptical pupil.

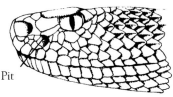

Pit

Underside of Tails

Note **single** row of subcaudals representative of pitvipers

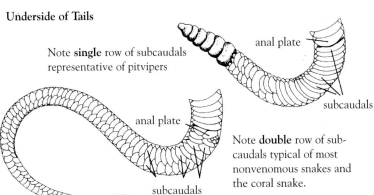

anal plate

subcaudals

anal plate

subcaudals

Note **double** row of subcaudals typical of most nonvenomous snakes and the coral snake.

The Genus Agkistrodon

Snakes of the *Agkistrodon* complex—35 species and sub-species in at least four genera—are considered to include some of the most primitive of the pitvipers. The name *Agkistrodon* is from a Greek combination meaning "hooked tooth," undoubtedly referring to the enlarged front fangs. The most recent evidence suggests that the genus itself originated in the New World, following dispersal of ancient pitviper stock across the Bering Land Bridge during the Late Oligocene/Early Miocene transition (about 25 million years ago); diversification into the forms we recognize today took place by the end of the latter epoch—about 7 million years ago. The current New World distribution includes the southeastern third of the United States, its northern boundary being southern New England, and its western edge being Kansas, extending in a disjunct fashion southward through Mexico, where it is primarily found along both coasts, to Costa Rica.

The two species of the genus which occur in Texas are the Copperhead and the Cottonmouth.

Copperhead

Scientific Name: *Agkistrodon contortrix* (Linnaeus, 1766).
Subspecies: Five subspecies are recognized. Three of these occur in Texas—namely, the Southern Copperhead (*A. c. contortrix*), the Broad-banded Copperhead (*A. c. laticinctus*) and the Trans-Pecos Copperhead (*A. c. pictigaster*). The Latin name *contortrix* means "twisting" or "twister" and probably refers to the pattern along the back; the Latin name *laticinctus* means "broad band," again referring to the dorsal

pattern; the Latin name *pictigaster* means "painted belly," and refers to the extensive ventral pigmentation found in this subspecies.

Description: Copperheads are medium-sized, relatively robust pitvipers, with adult males typically 1.5–2' (450–600 mm) in length and females somewhat smaller. The largest verifiable record for the forms which occur in Texas was of an individual 4' 4" (1,321 mm) in length. Usually 23 (range = 21–25) scale rows are present at midbody (in the Trans-Pecos Copperhead, there are likely to be 21 or 22 rows) (see p. 38 for how to count scale rows); dorsal scales are moderately to weakly keeled but may be smooth, especially toward the front of the body. Ventrals number 138–156, with little sexual dimorphism; subcaudals number 37–62, with males averaging about three more than females. Subcaudals may show a tendency to be divided, especially toward the tail tip and in western populations. Nine symmetrically arranged plates lie anteriorly on top of the head, and are followed by numerous smaller scales (see p. 49).

The ground color in the Southern Copperhead is pale tan to reddish-tan, somewhat darker toward the midline. The top of the head is unmarked except for a small dark spot on each parietal scale. The face below the eyes and backward to the angle of the jaw is pale gray to silver gray in color, and is bordered by a darker postocular stripe with a distinct lower border and a diffuse upper border. The dorsal pattern consists of 10–18 reddish-brown hourglass-shaped markings, darker toward their margins, and which are narrow along the spine and wider on the sides. They have a tendency not to meet along the spine, where a pair may in fact be offset, creating a somewhat mosaic appearance. These dorsal markings do not reach the ventral scales, which are unmarked except for a series of more or less distinct dark blotches along their outer margins. In the Broad-banded Copperhead, the dorsal ground color is pale brown with fine stippling of

Southern Copperhead (*Agkistrodon contortrix contortrix*)

red, gray or black. The dorsal bands are wide and usually complete, dark brown to red-brown and usually with narrow light borders; they extend to, and usually run across, the ventral scales. The dorsal color hues of the Trans-Pecos Copperhead are somewhat richer, and often the head is brighter than the remainder of the body. The black belly blotches are expanded and fuse across the midline and extend onto the lower sides of the body, where they blend into the middle of the light dorsal body bands at their lower margins. The tail tip is bright yellow in newborns of all subspecies, fading with age.

Similar Species: Rattlesnakes (genera *Crotalus* and *Sistrurus*) have a rattle (even just a button) on the end of the tail. Cottonmouths *(Agkistrodon piscivorus)* are generally darker, have a more pointed snout, may possess a light band from below the eye backward to the angle of the mouth, and lack a loreal scale. Harmless colubrid snakes lack the facial pit and usually have rounded pupils and patterned heads; if they have elliptical pupils, as in the night snakes and lyre snakes (genera *Hypsiglena* and *Trimorphodon*), there is usually some type of pattern present on the top of the head.

Habitat: Copperheads occupy a wide variety of wooded habitats, from the hardwood bottomlands along major rivers in East Texas to willow-oak-walnut-hackberry woodlands, which often exist as isolated patches, in Trans-Pecos Texas. They can be found in open habitats such as vacant lots, old fields and other agricultural or suburban situations that are not too far from wooded habitats. The natural range of this species extends into drier habitats only along wooded water-courses or other similar corridors, such as the Cross-Timbers in north-central Texas.

Behavior: Copperheads are relatively shy and inoffensive unless provoked by being stepped on, prodded or otherwise disturbed. Copperheads do occasionally climb, but spend most of their time on the ground. Although partial to moist surroundings and able to swim, they are rarely found in the water. Individual snakes typically remain loosely coiled for several days in the same spot under a log or similar object, in the open at the base of a tree, on a rocky ledge, or at the edge of a patch of vegetation, waiting for prey or digesting a meal. Their color pattern provides superb camouflage in these situations, and most copperheads go undetected by the unobservant. Copperheads may be active throughout the year under suitable environmental conditions. In spring and fall they are generally active during the day, and switch

Broad-banded Copperhead *(Agkistrodon contortrix laticinctus)*

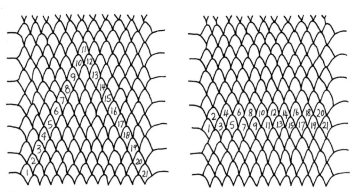

Two methods of counting the number of scale rows present at midbody
along a snake's back

to nocturnal activity during the summer when daytime temperatures become too warm. Copperheads will cease being surface-active during the winter if they cannot maintain body temperatures above 50°F (10°C), and they cannot tolerate body temperatures much above 77°F (25°C) during the summer.

Reproduction: Mating behavior in this species is very similar to that described for the Western Diamondback Rattlesnake (see p. 54). Males physically compete with each other for access to receptive females, and females may actively reject suitors defeated in such contests. Mating in Texas may occur most frequently in the spring or the fall, but can occur any time snakes are active. Females mating in the fall will not give birth until the following year, and some females store viable sperm for 2 years or more. Females may attain sexual maturity at 3 years of age or older and a length of about 18.5" (470 mm), although this can vary between individuals and is dependent on their ability to store sufficient energy reserves to support breeding activity. Pregnant females are sedentary for extended periods prior to giving birth, and may aggregate to do so. Litter size ranges from 2–15 and is positively correlated with female body size. Young are born in August and September and are about 6–8" (160–200 mm) in body length.

Food Habits: Copperheads are extremely catholic in diet, eating small rodents (voles, white-footed mice and harvest mice), shrews, small snakes (including occasionally their own kind), lizards, frogs and toads, salamanders and occasionally small birds and insects (caterpillars and cicadas). Prey selection is size-based, with larger snakes eating larger animals. Prey is hunted by ambush or by careful stalking behavior, and young copperheads may use their brightly colored tail tips to lure prey within striking distance. Copperheads themselves, especially young ones, fall victim to a wide variety of predators, including other snakes (coachwhips, indigo

Trans-Pecos Copperhead (*Agkistrodon contortrix pictigaster*)

snakes, kingsnakes, and racers), birds (hawks, owls, and roadrunners), and mammals (opossums, skunks, and weasels).

Venom Characteristics: Adult venom yields are typically 40–72 mg, with a maximum recorded yield of 148 mg (dry weight). Larger snakes produce more venom. Published LD_{50} values are in the range 6.5–10.5 mg/kg [i.p. (see glossary)], 10.92 mg/kg [i.v. (see glossary)], and 20.2–26.1 mg/kg [s.c. (see glossary)]. The lethal human dose is unknown, but has been estimated at 100 mg or more, with less than 0.5% of bites resulting in fatalities. Bites from this species should be

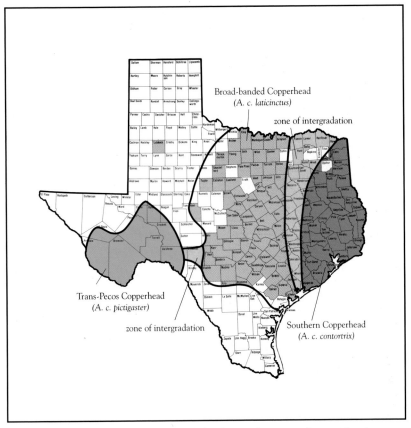

Broad-banded Copperhead
(A. c. laticinctus)

zone of intergradation

Trans-Pecos Copperhead
(A. c. pictigaster)

zone of intergradation

Southern Copperhead
(A. c. contortrix)

Known occurrence, by county, of the three subspecies of copperhead

taken seriously, but are generally not considered life-threatening because of the small yields and reduced lethality of the venom. Very few differences exist in venom characteristics between the subspecies. This venom differs from that of cottonmouths in that it possesses less hemolytic (red-blood-cell-destroying) activity. Copperheads possess blood serum factors which render them immune to their own venom and to that of cottonmouths.

Remarks: Males grow faster than females after about three years of age and reach a larger average size. The maximum lifespan documented for individuals of the three subspecies occurring in Texas exceeds twenty years in captivity, but copperheads in the wild rarely live more than ten years. The specimen record from Lubbock County (see map), outside the natural range of the species, resulted from an individual found within a load of cedar fence posts from Kerrville.

Cottonmouth

Scientific Name: *Agkistrodon piscivorus* (Lacépède, 1789). The Latin name *piscivorus* means "fish eating," and was given to this species because of its dietary characteristics.

Subspecies: Three subspecies are recognized; of these, one, the Western Cottonmouth *(A. p. leucostoma)*, occurs in Texas. The Latin name *leucostoma* means "white mouth," in reference to the feature which earned this species its common name.

Description: Cottonmouths are medium-sized, stout-bodied pitvipers, with adult males typically 20–30" (500–760 mm) in length and females somewhat smaller. The largest verifiable record for this subspecies is 5'2" (1,575 mm) in length. Usually 25 scale rows are present at midbody; the lowest scales may only be weakly keeled, and apical pits are present. Ventrals number 128–142, with little sexual dimorphism. Subcaudals number 36–53, with males averaging about 3 more than females, and show a tendency to be divided toward the tip of the tail. There are 9 symmetrically arranged plates anteriorly on top of the head, followed by numerous smaller scales (see p. 49).

The dorsal ground color is light-to-dark brown, and many adults are black. There are 10–15 complete or incomplete crossbands in patterned individuals, varying from only slightly darker than the ground color to black, and forming a series of spots where they extend onto the ventral surface.

The ventral surface is otherwise pale and without any markings except anteriorly, where it may be black. The head is brown or black, generally unmarked, and possesses a more or less distinct white stripe which extends backward from a point below the eye to the angle of the mouth. The pattern of newborn and juvenile snakes is sharp and distinct and fades with age, as does the light green or yellow color of the tail.

Similar Species: Rattlesnakes (genera *Crotalus* and *Sistrurus*) have a rattle (even if this is just a button) on the end of the tail. Copperheads *(Agkistrodon contortrix)* are generally light brown to reddish brown in color, have a more rounded snout, lack the light band below the eye backward to the angle of the mouth, and have a loreal scale. Harmless snakes lack the facial pit and usually have rounded pupils and patterned heads; if they have elliptical pupils, as in the night snakes and lyre snakes (genera *Hypsiglena* and *Trimorphodon*), there is usually some pattern on the top of the head. Harmless water snakes *(Nerodia* spp.), which are routinely mistaken for cottonmouths, can readily be distinguished by color, pattern and behavior. Water snakes have eyes which protrude beyond the supraocular scale, whereas the eyes of cottonmouths do not, giving the latter a scowling look. Also, when not stressed, cottonmouths swim with the head held higher out of the water than harmless water snakes do (see following page).

Habitat: Cottonmouths occupy a wide variety of aquatic and semiaquatic habitats, and are most abundant where prey is plentiful and environmental temperatures are not too extreme. They can be found in salt marshes, ponds, swamps and bayous, river bottomlands and streams that vary from muddy and sluggish to clear and fast-running. They require abundant basking sites, such as logs, brush piles and mud banks, and they also do well in urban areas. Cottonmouths occur upstream along major rivers (such as the Brazos and

Comparison of Western Cottonmouth with Harmless Water Snakes

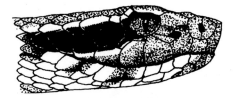

Western Cottonmouth

Green Water Snake

Yellow-bellied Water Snake
and Blotched Water Snake

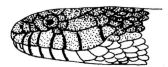

Diamondback Water Snake

Broad-banded Water Snake

Typical head elevation of an
unstressed swimming Western
Cottonmouth contrasted with a
nonvenomous water snake

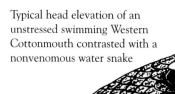

Western Cottonmouth

Harmless Water Snake

Colorado) and their tributaries into areas that would otherwise be too hot and dry to support them. Cottonmouths often travel far from water to hibernate.

Behavior: Much is made of the aggressiveness of cottonmouths, but their disposition is in fact similar to that of copperheads. Preferred body temperatures for activity lie between 64°F and 84°F (18°–29°C). They are good swimmers but are sluggish on land. When not engaged in hunting or reproductive activities, cottonmouths spend much of their time coiled at the edge of bodies of water or draped loosely in overhanging vegetation, often asleep. When disturbed in such situations, their first response is to drop into the water as quickly as possible; stories of cottonmouths ending up in canoes or johnboats are most likely a result of these vessels blocking the snake's intended escape route. Cottonmouths on land and away from a convenient escape route often give the defensive display which earned this species its common name. The head is held at the center of the coiled body and the mouth is gaped wide, revealing the milky white interior (harmless water snakes also have white mouths, but they do not exhibit this behavior). Often the tail is vigorously vibrated and a pungent musk emitted from scent glands at its base.

Reproduction: Typical male courtship behavior consists of jerky body movements when trailing the female, rapid flicking of the tongue and/or rubbing the chin on the female's back and repeated attempts at copulation while coiling his tail around hers. Courtship may occur in the water or on land, and courting males on land may challenge intruding males with characteristic pitviper dominance displays (the so-called "combat dance"). Mating in Texas usually occurs in the spring, but may take place at any time during the active season. Females probably attain sexual maturity at a minimum age of three years and a minimum body length of 18–20" (450–500 mm). Young are born alive

Adult Western Cottonmouth (*Agkistrodon piscivorus leucostoma*)

Young Western Cottonmouth (*Agkistrodon piscivorus leucostoma*)

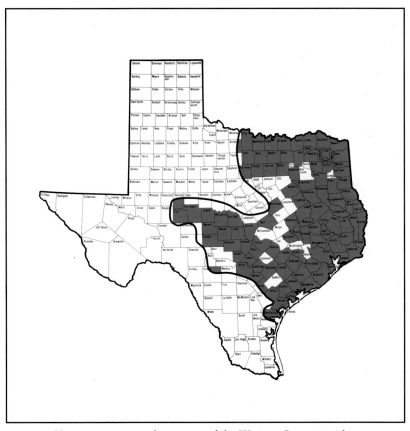

Known occurrence, by county, of the Western Cottonmouth
(Agkistrodon piscivorus leucostoma)

in late summer (July–September). Litter size averages 6 or 7, though it can range from 1 to 16, and is correlated with female body size. The mother may remain with her young for several days; she stays with them until they shed their skins for the first time.

Food Habits: Cottonmouth diets are as varied as those of copperheads, but differ in that they reflect the primarily aquatic habitats in which cottonmouths live. They can bite and inject venom underwater, and individuals are occasionally cannibalistic. Primary prey includes crayfish, fish (bass, catfish, killifish, minnows, perch and sunfish), salamanders, frogs and toads (cricket frogs, treefrogs, true frogs, spadefoot toads and true toads), lizards (green anoles and skinks), snakes (water snakes and garter and ribbon snakes), turtles (cooters and sliders), birds (Red-winged Blackbirds, cowbirds and meadowlarks) and small mammals (cotton rats, white-footed mice, harvest mice and shrews). Prey selection is size-based, with larger snakes eating larger prey. Hunting is by ambush or by careful stalking behavior. Young cottonmouths have bright yellow or green tail tips, which they employ to attract food items in a stereotyped behavior pattern called "caudal luring." This consists of juvenile snakes remaining motionless except for the tail tip, which is undulated back and forth in a fashion resembling the motion of a worm or insect larva. Potential prey, such as small lizards and frogs, can be lured within striking distance.

Cottonmouths themselves, especially young ones, fall victim to a wide variety of predators, including alligators, other snakes (racers and kingsnakes) and such birds as herons and egrets.

Venom Characteristics: Relatively little is known about the venom of this species. Adult venom yields are typically 90–170 mg dry weight. Published LD_{50} values include 5.11 mg/kg (i.p.), 4.00–4.17 mg/kg (i.v.) and 25.1 mg/kg (s.c.). The lethal human dose is unknown and undoubtedly variable, but it has been estimated at 100–150 mg. Cottonmouth venom differs from Copperhead venom in that it possesses considerable hemolytic (red-blood-cell-destroying) properties.

Remarks: Maximum lifespan for a captive individual of the Texas subspecies exceeded 21 years; natural lifespan is probably similar to that of copperheads.

The Rattlesnakes

Rattlesnakes are typical animals of the natural landscape of Texas, and are represented by at least one species in almost every county. They appeared relatively recently on the evolutionary stage as a group, with the oldest known fossils dating from the Pliocene, between 4 and 12 million years ago. There are two groups of rattlesnakes: The more primitive forms belong to the genus *Sistrurus* (three species, two of them found in Texas), and are characterized by a series of nine plates on the crown of the head similar to the arrangement found in the genus *Agkistrodon*. *Sistrurus* is distributed throughout the southeastern quarter of the United States, with disjunct populations in central Mexico. The more advanced forms of rattlesnakes belong to the genus *Crotalus* (at least twenty-eight species, six of them found in Texas). These have small scales covering the crown of the head. This genus occurs from Canada to Argentina, including a

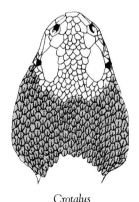

Sistrurus
(also *Agkistrodon*)

Crotalus

number of islands in the Sea of Cortéz and off the northern coast of South America. In addition to the characteristic features mentioned earlier for pitvipers, all but one rattlesnake species (an isolated island form in the Sea of Cortéz) possess the rattle. Both generic names are derived from Latin and refer to the possession of rattles on the tail—*Crotalus* comes from a word meaning "clapper" or "cymbal", while *Sistrurus* refers to "sistrum", a musical instument that rattles when shaken.

The rattle is a series of hollow, loosely interlocking segments of keratin—basically the same material of which fingernails are made. Contraction of a series of specialized shaker muscles in the tail causes these segments to vibrate against each other; the sound produced is amplified because they are hollow, and the intensity and other acoustic properties of the sound are dependent upon the size of the rattle. Contrary to popular belief, a rattlesnake's age cannot be determined by the number of segments of its rattle, because a new segment is added with each shedding of the snake's skin. Snakes shed their skins as part of the growth process, and will shed more often when they are younger and when food is plentiful. An individual rattlesnake may thus shed its skin 4–6 times annually during the first several years of life, and perhaps only once a year after reaching maturity. In addition, segments are frequently broken off as individuals encounter the hazards of their environment; as a result, older rattlesnakes with complete rattles are rarely seen. Even if all the rattle segments were to be accidentally lost, however, a rattlesnake's tail would end in a stump rather than in a gradual taper to a point, as is characteristic of all other snakes.

Rattlesnakes found in Texas are described on the following pages.

Western Diamondback Rattlesnake (*Crotalus atrox*)

Western Diamondback Rattlesnake

Scientific Name: *Crotalus atrox* Baird and Girard, 1853. The Latin name *atrox* means "savage," "fierce" or "cruel," probably in reference to this snake's imposing defensive display and venomous nature, and to the reactions of settlers and explorers moving west in the nineteenth century who first encountered this species.

Subspecies: No subspecies have been recognized.

Description: Western Diamondbacks are large rattlesnakes, with adults typically ranging from 2.5 to 4.5 ft. (760–1,370 mm) in length. The maximum recorded size is a male from Dallas County, Texas, at 7'8" (2,337 mm) in length. Adult males are about 10% larger than females of the same age. There are 23–29 (usually 25) keeled scale rows at midbody. Males have 168–193 ventral scales and 19–32 subcaudals; corresponding counts in females are, respectively, 173–196 and 16–36. There are 11–32 small scales on the crown of the head between the snout and the eyes, and 3–8 intersupraocular scales.

The ground color is brown to gray, although certain populations may be reddish, yellowish or blackish, depending on the prevailing substrate. The dorsal pattern consists of 24–45 dark diamond-shaped markings or irregular hexagons with light borders that are somewhat indistinct because their scales are not uniform in color. A series of indistinct lateral dark markings extends along each side. The tail is distinctly marked with black-and-white bands (thus the vernacular name, "coon-tail") which are approximately equal in width, and number 4–16. A pair of distinct white stripes, one starting from in front of the eye and the other from behind it, run in parallel downward and backward to the mouth; the posterior stripe makes contact with the mouth well in front of the angle of the jaw.

Similar Species: The species in Texas most likely to be confused with the Western Diamondback is the Mojave Rattlesnake. The latter species has larger scales on the top of the head (1–2, rarely 3 intersupraoculars), the black tail bands are usually much narrower than the white ones, and the posterior white stripe on the side of the head extends backward above the angle of the mouth (see p.74 under Mojave Rattlesnake).

Habitat: The Western Diamondback can be found in virtually every dryland habitat within its range, although it seems to prefer habitats that are neither too closed nor too

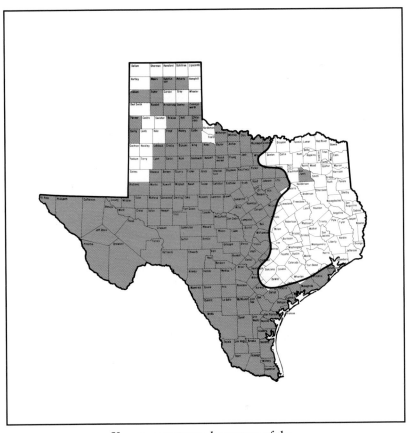

**Known occurrence, by county, of the
Western Diamondback Rattlesnake** (*Crotalus atrox*)

open. Thus it is uncommon in dense woodland or short-grass prairie. Habitats in which Western Diamondbacks may be especially abundant include rocky canyons, such as those cutting into the caprock escarpment of the Panhandle, the Edwards and Stockton Plateaus of west-central Texas, the creosotebush deserts of far west Texas, the mesquite-savannahs of south Texas, and the dunes and coastal barrier islands along the Gulf Coast.

Behavior: Western Diamondbacks are active all year long in southern Texas; even individuals from more northern populations which overwinter in dens may be active around them for extended periods on warm days. Western Diamondbacks typically leave their winter dens between March and May, when daylong temperatures become warm enough, and migrate to their summer ranges. Migration distances can be up to several kilometers, and home ranges as large as 22 acres (9 hectares). During the warm summer months, Western Diamondbacks are active largely at night, although they may continue their activity into early morning hours before it gets too hot. Preferred body temperatures for activity are 75°–86°F (24°–30°C). As day length shortens and night-time temperatures cool in the late summer, Western Diamondbacks increase their amount of daytime activity and begin their migration to winter den sites. The mechanisms used to navigate their way are largely unknown, but are thought to involve chemical and solar cues, along with geographic landmarks.

When disturbed, these snakes are quick to assume the well-known defensive posture immortalized in the minds of so many generations of people through books, stories, movies, TV shows and postcards found in virtually every traveler's stop in western America. The striking pose has the head and front part of the body held high and retracted in an S-shaped coil directly over the rest of the body, which is anchored firmly to the ground. The rattle is shaken vigorously and the tongue extended repeatedly, often held for a second or two while curved backward over the top of the head. This posture can be held indefinitely, as long as the snake continues to perceive a threat to its safety. It is important to recognize this behavior as strictly defensive on the part of the snake, however; should the threat not escalate (if, for example, the threatening object stands still or retreats), the intensity of the display will slowly diminish and the snake will move away to seek safety.

Reproduction: Mating most often takes place in the spring following emergence from winter hibernation, but it may also occur throughout the summer and into the fall. A male actively courts a female, using tactile and chemical cues; it slowly approaches her, rubs its chin along her back while flicking its tongue rapidly and exhibits precise body movements. Females will move off if not ready to mate, but if receptive, they will move very little and the actual copulation may last for as long as 24 hours. The mating season is also the time when snake "dancing" is observed. This behavior involves two snakes twisting together and raising the front half of their bodies off the ground. These "dances" almost always involve two males engaged in a struggle for dominance, regardless of whether a female is actually present.

Females attain sexual maturity at three years of age and at about 3 feet (900 mm) in length. Diamondbacks in northern and central Texas may only reproduce once every two years, whereas those in south Texas may do so annually. Litter size is correlated with female body size, and averages about 14 young, with a maximum of 25 reported. They are born from July through September, again depending on geographic location. Neonates are about 14" (360 mm) in length and grow rapidly during their first year; most growth occurs during the first four years of life. Individual females may travel long distances from their summer ranges to give birth, and are known to remain in close proximity to their newborn young for up to a week, at least until the young shed their skins for the first time.

Food Habits: Diet consists primarily of small mammals. Larger snakes prefer prey such as cottontails, ground squirrels, woodrats and kangaroo rats, whereas smaller individuals take smaller prey, such as pocket mice, white-footed mice and harvest mice. Small birds and lizards are occasionally eaten. When prey is scarce, they may scavenge for dead food items. Western Diamondbacks, especially young ones, have a long list of enemies, including other snakes (coachwhips, indigo snakes, kingsnakes and whipsnakes), birds (hawks, owls and roadrunners) and various mammals (skunks, badgers, coyotes and foxes).

Venom Characteristics: Adult venom yields are large,

averaging 400 mg (dry weight), with a maximum recorded yield of 1,150 mg. The fangs are relatively long, measuring 0.4–0.5" (10–13 mm) in adults. Average i.p. LD_{50} values (mg/kg) have been shown to vary from 1.0 in young (8 months old) to 5.0 (range = 3.7–8.4) in adults. Other published LD_{50} ranges are 3.71–13.6 (i.p.), 1.0–6.3 (i.v.) and 16–19 (s.c.) mg/kg. The average lethal human dose is unknown and undoubtedly variable, but it has been estimated at approximately 100 mg of venom. Western Diamondback venom possesses high proteolytic and anticoagulant activity, but individuals of this species possess blood-borne factors which confer immunity to the hemorrhagic effects of conspecific venom. A number of potential mammalian predator and prey species, including opossums, raccoons, woodrats and ground squirrels, possess similar factors, conferring varying degrees of immunity.

Remarks: Captive individuals have lived as long as 30 years. Annual mortality in the wild is reported to be about 20%; rarely, individuals in the wild may live to be 15 years old.

Timber Rattlesnake

Scientific Name: *Crotalus horridus* Linnaeus, 1758. The Latin name *horridus* means "horrible" or "dreadful," a reference to the snake's venomous nature and the reactions to it of the first European colonists in the northeastern United States.

Subspecies: No subspecies are recognized (see **Remarks**).

Description: Timber Rattlesnakes are large rattlesnakes; adult males average about 4'3" (1,310 mm) and 3.75 pounds (1,700 gm), while adult females average 3'11" (1,200 mm) and 2.9 pounds (1,300 gm) in some southern populations. The largest specimen ever measured was 6'3" (1,892 mm) in length. Dorsal scale rows at midbody number 23 or 24

Timber Rattlesnake (*Crotalus horridus*)

(range = 21–26) and are keeled. Males have 158–177 ventral scales and 20–30 subcaudals; corresponding counts in females are 163–183 ventrals and 13–26 subcaudals. The scales between the supraoculars are small, numerous and arranged in 5–8 irregular longitudinal rows.

The ground color varies from yellow to black and may include shades of brown, tan or gray. The dorsal pattern consists of 15–34 dark transverse chevron or irregularly V-shaped markings. The sooty-brown or black coloration of the tail may extend forward on the body some distance, and may obscure the posterior transverse bands. Most Texas specimens have a distinct reddish or orange vertebral stripe, 1–4 scales wide, which extends from the neck backward to the tail. The snout and crown of the head may have considerable dark brown or black pigmentation, and a brown stripe 2–3 scales wide may extend from the posterior edge of the eye downward to the angle of the mouth or slightly beyond.

Similar Species: The only other species of rattlesnake native to Texas with an entirely black tail is the Blacktail Rattlesnake, but in that species the black coloration is restricted to the tail and does not extend forward onto the body. In addition, the Blacktail Rattlesnake lacks a reddish or orange vertebral stripe and transverse dorsal chevron markings. The scales on the crown of the head in the Timber Rattlesnake are smaller and more numerous than in the Blacktail Rattlesnake. The dorsal processes of the vertebrae of the Timber Rattlesnake are enlarged compared with those of the Blacktail Rattlesnake, giving it a more pronounced ridged backbone.

Habitat: Timber Rattlesnakes, as the name suggests, occupy forested areas of central and eastern Texas, such as the Cross Timbers, bottomland hardwoods and pine woodlands. Most individuals prefer areas with 50% or more closed canopies and thick ground vegetation, but pregnant females will seek out more open habitats, where they spend considerable time basking, thereby elevating body temperatures and enhancing gestation. Home range sizes may be as large as 494 acres (200 hectares) for males. Water is not a barrier; radio-telemetered individuals in Nacogdoches County are known to have crossed the Angelina River.

Behavior: A relatively mild-tempered species; individuals depend upon the ability of their pattern to blend in with the environment as their first line of defense. Males travel greater linear distances than females within their home ranges, especially during the breeding season. At this time males may move more than a mile per week, covering areas

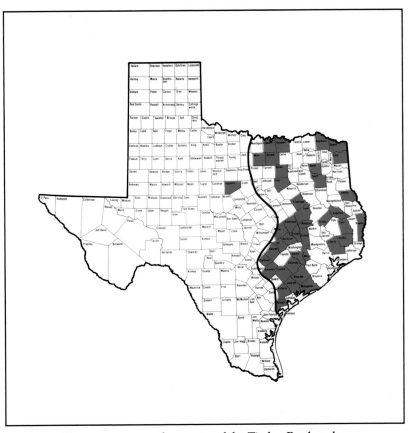

Known occurrence, by county, of the Timber Rattlesnake
(Crotalus horridus)

over a mile in diameter, in search of females. Extended periods may be spent in centers of activity, which usually comprise less than 10% of an individual's home range. Except for pregnant females, which are rather sedentary, individuals may shift their centers of activity throughout their home ranges as the seasons progress.

Reproduction: Little is known about the reproductive habits of this species in Texas. Females in northern populations may not reproduce until they are nine or ten years old, and then they produce a litter only once every three or four years. Since the active season in Texas is longer than it is farther north, it can be inferred that females attain sexual maturity at an earlier age and reproduce more frequently in Texas. Males and females from Kansas and South Carolina attain sexual maturity at about 3'3" (1,000 mm) in length, which is when females are three years old (Kansas) or four years old (South Carolina), and when males are 6 years old (South Carolina). Females may reproduce only every second or third year after that. Mating activity in Texas occurs in late summer and continues until snakes move to hibernacula in the fall. Females presumably store sperm until spring activity resumes. Litter size ranges from 5 to 16. The young snakes, born in late summer to early fall, range from 11 to 17" (290–430 mm) in length.

Food Habits: Timber Rattlesnakes are ambush predators, often lying for long periods of time in an S-shaped coil with the head perpendicular to pathways, such as the long axis of a fallen log, actively used by small mammals. These snakes eat a wide variety of such prey, including white-footed mice, cotton rats, squirrels and rabbits.

Venom Characteristics: Venom yields are large in adults, averaging 140 mg (with a range of 95–150), and with a maximum dry weight of 300 mg. The fangs are relatively long, averaging 0.35–0.43" (9–11 mm) in adults. As with the Western Diamondback Rattlesnake and the Western Rattlesnake, the potency of the venom appears to be higher in newborns than in adults. Recent research indicates polymorphism in venom types in this species, with venoms characterized as primarily neurotoxic, as primarily hemorrhagic, as exhibiting both of these properties, or as exhibiting neither. Canebrake toxin, a bipolar molecule with a minimum molecular weight of about 23,000 daltons, greatly enhances the lethality of any venom type. LD_{50} values (i.p.) from specimens caught in the wild and possessing primarily neurotoxic venoms with canebrake toxin are 0.22–1.0 mg/kg; for hemorrhagic venoms lacking canebrake toxin, the LD_{50} values (i.p.) are 2.2–8.0 mg/kg; and for venoms possessing both properties, the LD_{50} values (i.p.) are 1.3–1.9 mg/kg. All three venom types may occur in Texas. In another study, an average LD_{50} value (i.p.) averaging 0.4 mg/kg (with a range of 0.3–0.5) was recorded for the most toxic venom type. Corresponding values for the least toxic variety of Timber Rattlesnake venom average 5.3 mg/kg (with a range of 4.0–6.6). Other published lethality values for this species are an LD_{50} value of 2.91 mg/kg (i.p.), 2.63 mg/kg (i.v.) and 2.25–15.63 mg/kg (s.c.). The lethal human dose is unknown and undoubtedly variable, but has been estimated at 75–100 mg of venom. This venom exhibits high 5'-nucleotidase and hyaluronidase activities (see glossary).

Remarks: For many years, southern populations were considered a distinct subspecies—namely, the Canebrake Rattlesnake (*C. h. atricaudatus*). The weight of current evidence suggests that this is a subjective distinction; there appear to be no geographically coherent genetic or morphological patterns throughout the range of this species that would support this classification. Rather, it appears that the species reinvaded its northern range from southern refuge areas following the last glacial period in North America about 10,000 years ago. Whether this resulted in population divergence warranting taxonomic recognition remains to be determined.

Northern populations, particularly those in New England, are in serious trouble from long-term prosecution and habitat destruction combined with a life-history pattern of late-maturing individuals producing few offspring. The species enjoys some form of protection in most of these states, but the efficacy of these measures remains to be determined. This species is protected in Texas, where it is listed as a threatened species. Natural longevities are unknown, but a captive individual from Texas lived more than 30 years.

Mottled Rock Rattlesnake *(Crotalus lepidus lepidus)*

Rock Rattlesnake

Scientific Name: *Crotalus lepidus* (Kennicott, 1861). The Latin name *lepidus* means "pretty" or "attractive," in reference to the color pattern.

Subspecies: Four subspecies are recognized, of which two occur in the United States: the Mottled Rock Rattlesnake (*C. l. lepidus*) and the Banded Rock Rattlesnake (*C. l. klauberi*); both can be found in Texas. The Latin subspecies

Banded Rock Rattlesnake (*Crotalus lepidus klauberi*)

name *klauberi* is a patronym for Laurence Klauber, the foremost authority in the scientific study of rattlesnakes.

Description: Rock Rattlesnakes are small and relatively slender, with adult males typically 15–20" (380–500 mm) in length and females somewhat smaller. The largest verifiable record was of an individual measuring 2'9" (828 mm) in length. Scale rows at midbody number 21–26 and there are 14–24 scales on top of the head, between and in front of the eyes. Males have 147–172 ventral and 20–33 subcaudal scales; corresponding counts in females are 149–170 and 16–24. The rattle is large and well-developed in proportion

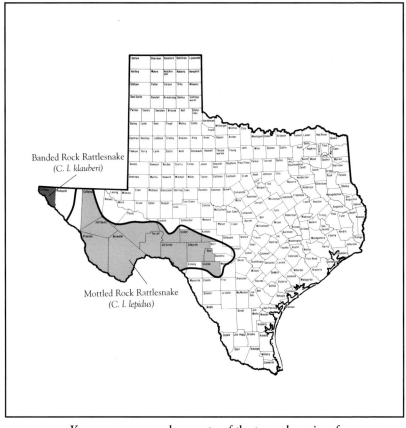

**Known occurrence, by county, of the two subspecies of
Rock Rattlesnake** (*Crotalus lepidus*)

to the body. The basic ground color varies considerably with
geographic location, and individuals within a population
tend to match the background coloration of the rocks on
which they live (although individuals are incapable of
changing color during their lifetimes). Newborn snakes have
yellow tails of varying hues which fade as they age; the head
and tail of an adult is the same color as its body. These colors include chalky white, buff, tan, pink, red, green, blue-
gray and sometimes almost black. Some populations of the
Banded Rock Rattlesnake exhibit sexual dichromatism;
males are basically green dorsally and females are gray with

more mottling. This phenomenon, however, has not been reported in Texas populations. Superimposed upon the ground color is a dorsal pattern of 15–25 narrow dark brown or black crossbands, without light borders, which start behind the head and extend onto the tail. Individuals of the subspecies *lepidus* have 1–3 indistinct crossbands between each pair of primary bands, giving them a mottled appearance, and they possess a dark stripe extending backward from each eye to the corner of the mouth. Individuals of the subspecies *klauberi* (found in El Paso and Culberson counties) lack the secondary crossbands and the dark stripe from the eye, and have a pair of light-brown-to-black blotches on the back of the head. There is a broad zone of intergradation between these subspecies in west Texas, within which individuals may possess some combination of these as well as other scale characteristics. The color of the belly varies from white to gray, with small gray or brown blotches or flecks, especially toward the sides and tail.

Similar Species: The combination of small size, vertically divided upper preocular scale, relatively well-developed rattle and color pattern will distinguish this species from others native to Texas.

Habitat: This species is an inhabitant of rough terrain, such as rocky canyons, boulder fields and talus slopes. It occurs from elevations as low as 1,155 feet (350 m) along the Pecos River and Rio Grande valleys to elevations as high as 8,580 feet (2,600 m) in the Guadalupe mountains of west Texas. Characteristic vegetation types within occupied habitat include xeric desert forms such as acacia, agave, sotol and yucca to juniper, pinyon and oak communities at higher or more sheltered sites. This species may be abundant in a given area, but individuals are seldom seen because of their behavior. The Rock Rattlesnake, more than any other species of rattlesnake in Texas, tends to occur in isolated populations separated from others by unsuitable or unoccupied terrain.

Behavior: These snakes are shy and secretive, well-camouflaged and rarely seen by the casual observer; they will bite readily, however, if disturbed. They frequently spend their active time on the surface hidden in cracks and crevices, under rocks or rock ledges or sheltered by vegetation. There are two primary activity periods during the summer, one from about 6 a.m. to 10 a.m. and another from 6 p.m. to midnight; these periods can be lengthened or shortened by environmental conditions such as rainfall or drought.

Reproduction: Extended ritualized combat between males occurs in this species and, as in other viperids, appears to be a contest between individuals for social dominance. Litter size is correlated with female body size, and ranges from 2 to 6. Individual females can reproduce every year if they can eat enough food and sequester sufficient energy reserves. Their young are born as early as July.

Food Habits: These snakes are ambush predators, often lying motionless in an S-shaped coil, waiting for prey to move within striking distance. Lizards, including whiptails, spiny lizards, Greater Earless Lizards and Tree Lizards, are the favorite prey. Small rodents, such as pocket mice and white-footed mice, are readily eaten, as are centipedes. Small snakes and arthropods, such as grasshoppers, are occasionally eaten, the latter especially by young individuals. Young snakes use their yellow tails as lures to attract prey within striking distance.

Venom Characteristics: Venom yields from adults are small; from limited data, they appear to range from 5 to 25 mg, with a maximum of 33 mg (dry weight). Published LD_{50} values are 0.38–5.0 mg/kg (i.p.), 9.0 mg/kg (i.v.) and 11.55–23.95 mg/kg (s.c.). There is considerable variation in venom biochemistry, which appears to be related to geographic distribution. The fangs are relatively short, ranging from 0.12–0.16" (3–4 mm) in adults.

Remarks: Maximum reported longevities for captive individuals are over 17 years for *C. l. lepidus* and 23 years for *C. l. klauberi*. I have an individual *C. l. lepidus*, collected in west Texas as an adult, which has lived in my collection for 21 years.

Blacktail Rattlesnake

Scientific Name: *Crotalus molossus* (Baird and Girard, 1853). The Latin name *molossus* refers to the Molossian hound of antiquity; the etymology is obscure, but it may be due to an old and little-used common name for this species—namely, the Dog-faced Rattlesnake.

Subspecies: Three subspecies are recognized; of these, the Northern Blacktail Rattlesnake *(C. m. molossus)* occurs in Texas.

Description: Blacktails are medium-sized rattlesnakes, with adults typically ranging from 2.5' to 3' (800–900 mm) in length. The largest specimen on record is a male measuring 4'4" (1,330 mm) in length. The head is relatively large in proportion to the body, and there is a marked tendency for the scales between the supraoculars to be relatively large and few (4–12) in number. There are on average 27 dorsal scale rows (with a range of 23–31) at midbody, all keeled except for the lowest 1–4 on each side. There are 166–199 ventral scales and 22–30 subcaudals in males; the corresponding counts in females are 177–201 and 16–25. The scales on the side of the head tend to be subdivided, resulting in a relatively high number of labials, loreals and prefoveals (see glossary).

This may be the most attractive rattlesnake in North America. A great deal of individual and geographic variation in ground color exists, from yellow through olive-green and greenish-gray to almost black. The dorsal pattern consists of 20–41 brown or red-brown rhomboids bordered by light unicolored scales, and there may be small groups of such scales scattered within the dark rhomboids. There is a lateral series of similar markings on each side. The light borders of all three series may be united, especially toward the tail, forming very irregular crossbands. The tail and rattle are uniformly black. The snout and head in front of the eyes are dark brown to black, and a dark brown band 3–4 scales wide extends from the rear of the eye downward to the angle of the mouth.

Similar Species: The only other species of rattlesnake native to Texas with an entirely black tail is the Timber Rattlesnake, but in that species the black coloration extends forward on the body for some distance. Further, the Blacktail Rattlesnake lacks the vertebral orange stripe and the transverse dorsal bands or chevron markings of the Timber Rattlesnake. The scales on the crown of the head in the Blacktail Rattlesnake are larger and fewer in number than in the Timber Rattlesnake. In addition, the dorsal processes of the vertebrae of the Blacktail Rattlesnake are reduced in comparison with those of the Timber Rattlesnake, giving the former a less pronounced ridged backbone.

Habitat: This is a species of rocky roughland habitats in xeric or semi-xeric areas throughout its range. It is uncommon on the Edwards Plateau, seemingly confined to narrow, well-vegetated canyons, sinkholes and similar features. In west Texas it can be found in all suitable habitats, but is most common from foothills and bajadas (see glossary) with native bunchgrasses, ocotillo, yucca and acacia at about 4,100' (1,240 m), through pine-oak woodlands at about 8,500' (2,576 m).

Behavior: This is probably the most docile species of the genus in Texas; individuals rarely rattle unless directly disturbed, but rather depend on their striking color and pattern characteristics, which provide superb camouflage within the roughland habitats they occupy. Individuals may travel as much as 13.6 miles (22 km) during an activity season and have home ranges as large as 15 acres (6 hectares). Blacktails may be active all year long and at temperatures as low as 50°F

Northern Blacktail Rattlesnake (*Crotalus molossus molossus*)

(10°C), although most activity takes place from March through October at preferred body temperatures of about 86°F (30°C).

Reproduction: Very little is known about this species. Males may accompany females for several weeks in the field during the summer. Mating occurs in late summer or early fall, which is also the time when male–male combat most frequently occurs. Females store sperm until spring emergence; ovulation and fertilization take place at this time. The young are born in July or August in litters of 8–10, at a size of 9–11" (230–280 mm). Females may give birth in communal rookeries, and remain with the young until the

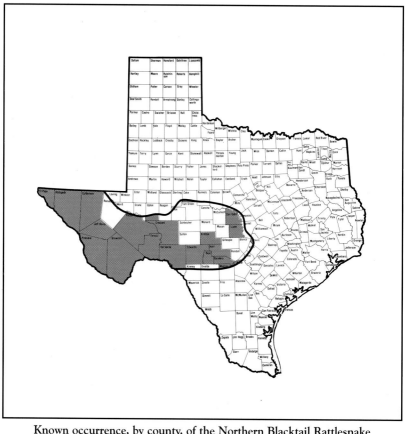

Known occurrence, by county, of the Northern Blacktail Rattlesnake
(Crotalus molossus molossus)

latter have shed their skins for the first time.

Food Habits: Although data are few, newborn and young blacktails probably prey upon small mammals such as shrews, pocket mice and white-footed mice, as well as lizards like the Canyon Spiny Lizard, the Crevice Spiny Lizard and the Tree Lizard, which are abundant within occupied habitat. Adult snakes eat larger mammals, such as rabbits, squirrels, woodrats, kangaroo rats and occasionally ground-nesting birds or those which nest low to the ground. The largest prey may provide an individual snake with up to one-third of its basic metabolic requirements for an activity season. Like other species of rattlesnake, individual black-tails seek out places in which they can bask after eating, thereby raising their body temperature as much as 9°F (5°C) higher than it is in the non-feeding condition, in order to aid digestion.

Venom Characteristics: Limited data show venom yields from adults to be moderate, averaging 180–286 mg (dry weight), with a maximum of 540 mg. As with other species, there are significant individual and age-related differences in venom properties, with important biomedical implications. An LD_{50} range of 2.7–7.0 mg/kg (i.p.) has been reported. The venom has strong anticoagulant properties and high protease activities. The fangs are relatively long, at 0.39–0.55" (10–14 mm) in adults.

Remarks: Natural lifespans are unknown, but a captive adult from Texas lived more than 20 years.

Mojave Rattlesnake

Scientific Name: *Crotalus scutulatus* (Kennicott, 1861). The Latin name *scutulatus* means "diamond- or lozenge-shaped," and refers to the dorsal color pattern.

Subspecies: Two subspecies are recognized; one of these, the Mojave Rattlesnake (*C. s. scutulatus*), occurs in Texas.

Description: Mojaves are medium-sized and somewhat slender, with adults ranging from 2' to 3' (600–900 mm) in length. Maximum recorded size is 4'6" (1,372 mm) for a male from Brewster County. There are 21–29 scale rows at midbody and 8–23 scales on top of the head from the nose to the level of the eyes. The scales between the supraoculars in the Mojave Rattlesnake are relatively large and lie in only 2–3 rows. Males have 165–190 ventral and 21–29 subcaudal scales; corresponding counts in females are 167–192 ventral and 15–25 subcaudal scales.

Mojave Rattlesnake (*Crotalus scutulatus scutulatus*)

The dorsal ground color can be various shades or combinations of green, yellow, olive, gray or brown. A wide, poorly defined dark stripe extends from each eye downward and backward to the angle of the mouth, with a well-defined light stripe bordering the dark one posteriorly, and extending backward above the angle of the mouth. The dorsal pattern consists of 24–36 dark-gray-to-brown blotches, usually diamond-shaped but occasionally oval to hexagonal, each with an exterior border of uniformly light-colored scales one scale wide. The tail is distinctly banded with black and white

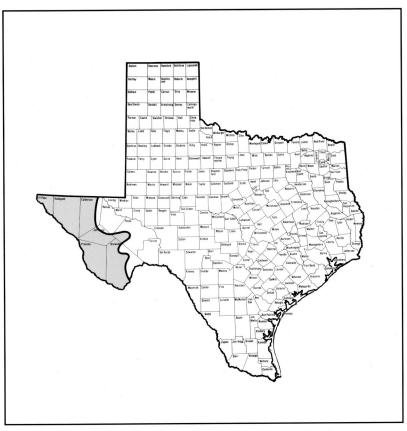

Known occurrence, by county, of the Mojave Rattlesnake
(Crotalus scutulatus scutulatus)

rings, the white ones up to three times as wide as the black. The lower half of the basal rattle segment is usually much lighter in color than the remainder of the rattle.

Similar Species: The only other species native to Texas with a distinctively black-and-white banded tail is the Western Diamondback Rattlesnake. The latter species has smaller scales on the top of the head (rarely three, usually four or more intersupraoculars); additionally, in the Western Diamondback, the light postocular stripe extends downward to before or at the angle of the mouth, and the black and

Mojave Rattlesnake

Western Diamondback Rattlesnake

white tail bands are approximately equal in width.

Habitat: This species occurs in open creosotebush desert flats and desert grasslands, generally without rocky soils, at elevations below 5,000' (1,515 m).

Behavior: This species is almost always nocturnal during the summer months, but can be found during the day at other times during its activity season, which extends from March through October. It has a reputation for being highly aggressive, and this characteristic, if accurate, combined with the increased toxicity of its venom, would place this species at the high end of the danger scale. Fortunately, however, this reputation is overstated; individuals are just as likely to attempt to escape as they are to assume the characteristic defensive posture of congeners (see glossary) such as the Western Diamondback Rattlesnake. Individuals hibernate singly or in small groups, and may be active at the mouth of hibernacula (see glossary) on warm days.

Reproduction: Very little is known about this species. Mating may take place at any time during the summer activity season. Females inseminated late during the season may store sperm for use in fertilizing ova following spring emergence from hibernation. The young snakes are born from July through September, with a peak in August. Litter size averages about 9, with a range of 5–13.

Food Habits: Although juveniles may take a wide variety of prey, from insects to small mammals, adults primarily eat mammals. Such prey items include kangaroo rats, pocket mice, white-footed mice, ground squirrels and rabbits.

Venom Characteristics: The fangs are relatively short, ranging from 0.28" to 0.35" (7–9 mm) in adults. Venom yields from adults are moderate, averaging 70 (with a range of 50–90), and with a maximum of 150 mg dry weight. There are distinct biochemical and toxicological differences in venoms from different populations throughout the geographic range of this species; the Texas population has the more toxic venom. These populations exhibit considerable neurotoxic activity in their venom, with little local edema or tissue damage but significant systemic effects resulting from bites. An average LD_{50} value (i.p.) of 0.24 (ranging from 0.13 to 0.54) mg/kg has been reported for the most toxic venom variety. Comparable values for a less toxic venom variant are 3.0 (range = 2.3–3.8) mg/kg. Additional LD_{50} values reported are 0.12–0.21 mg/kg (i.v.) and 0.31 mg/kg (s.c.). The lethal human dose is unknown and undoubtedly variable, but has been estimated at 10–15 mg. The venom is devoid of hemorrhagic and high alkaline phosphomonoesterase activities. This is generally recognized as one of the most dangerous species of rattlesnake in North America because of its relatively large size, the irritable tendency of certain individuals and the potency of the venom.

Remarks: Natural longevities are unknown for this species. A captive individual, still alive at the time of the survey, was 14 years old.

Western Rattlesnake

Scientific Name: *Crotalus viridis* (Rafinesque, 1818). The Latin name *viridis* means "green," in reference to a typical ground color in this form.

Subspecies: Nine subspecies are recognized, of which one, the Prairie Rattlesnake (*C. v. viridis*), occurs in Texas.

Description: Prairie Rattlesnakes are medium-sized and relatively slender, with adults measuring 2'8"–3'10" (812–1,168 mm) in length. The largest recorded specimen was 4'11.75" (1,515 mm) in length. There are on average 27 scale rows at midbody (ranging from 23 to 29), and these scales are keeled. Males have 164–189 ventral and 21–31 subcaudal scales; the corresponding counts in females are 170–196 and 14–26. There are 4 internasal scales in contact with the rostral scale (see glossary). The ground color is usually tan or light brown, but can be greenish-gray, olive-green or greenish-brown. The dorsal pattern consists of 33–57 squarish dark brown blotches with narrow but distinct white borders; the blotches tend to become less distinct, forming crossbands, and the white borders tend to disappear toward the tail. The tail is banded, but not in black and white; there are 6–15 brown bands in males and 4–11 in females. Up to three series of indistinct lateral body blotches may occur. Two white flash marks occur on each side of the face, one extending from in front of the eye downward to the line of the mouth, and the other extending from behind the eye backward above the angle of the jaw.

Similar Species: The Western Diamondback Rattlesnake and the Mojave Rattlesnake both have distinct black-and-white-banded tails, distinct dorsal diamond-shaped (rather than square-shaped) markings on at least the front part of the body and only two (rather than four) internasal scales touching the rostral scale. The Massasauga has nine large plates

Prairie Rattlesnake *(Crotalus viridis viridis)*

instead of many small scales covering the crown of the head.

Habitat: A general and ubiquitous inhabitant of grass-lands throughout its range, the Prairie Rattlesnake can characteristically be found associated with ground-squirrel and prairie-dog colonies within the High Plains, Rolling Plains and Trans-Pecos natural regions of Texas, where it utilizes these animals for food and their burrows for shelter. It is less commonly encountered within escarpment breaks, flood-plains and desert scrub, habitats more frequently occupied by congeners such as the Western Diamondback Rattlesnake.

Behavior: Both male and non-pregnant female snakes leave winter den sites in the spring and may travel 4.3 miles

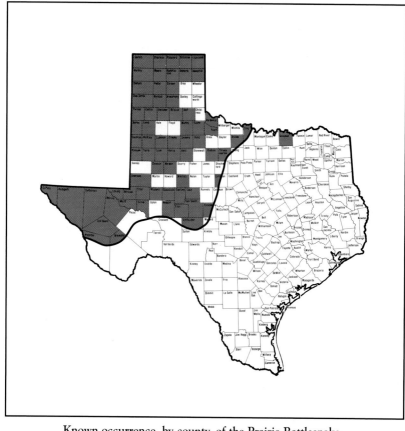

Known occurrence, by county, of the Prairie Rattlesnake
(Crotalus viridis viridis)

(7 km) or more until they reach areas of relatively high prey densities, where individual snakes may remain for the first half of the summer. Females continue to search out prey patches after that, whereas males begin to search for females with which to mate in the latter part of the summer. Snakes seek out hibernacula in which to spend the winter when body temperatures fall below about 84°F (29°C), often returning to the same one year after year. Individuals may remain active in the den throughout the winter, and may bask at the entrance on warm days, as long as body temper-

ature can be maintained at about 52°F (11°C).

Reproduction: Little is known about the reproductive habits of this species in Texas. Elsewhere, mating takes place from late summer into fall, and mated females store sperm throughout the winter. Males are active during the spring while replenishing energy reserves, and warm body temperatures are required to initiate the annual sperm-production cycle. Pregnant females leave the winter den in the spring and travel short distances to specific birthing areas called rookeries. Here they remain relatively sedentary, feed little, maintain elevated body temperatures to aid gestation, and give birth in the late summer or early fall. Several dozen females may congregate in the same rookery. Litter size is correlated with female body size, and averages about 9 young (with a range of 5–14). Newborn snakes are able to follow scent trails of adults to find overwintering den sites.

Food Habits: In addition to the rodents mentioned above, gophers, kangaroo rats, woodrats, pocket mice and white-footed mice form the bulk of the diet. Ground-dwelling birds may also be taken, and lizards such as whiptails, earless lizards, fence lizards and side-blotched lizards are routinely eaten by young snakes. Tongue-flicking rates are greatly enhanced after snakes strike prey objects. This behavior helps a snake use chemical cues to find envenomated prey, which may have traveled some distance prior to death.

Venom Characteristics: Venom yields from adults are moderate, averaging 44 mg (range = 25–100), with a maximum of 165 mg dry weight. Reported LD_{50} values are 1.1–1.61 mg/kg (i.v.), 1.25–2.3 mg/kg (i.p.) and 5.5–14.8 mg/kg (s.c.). As with the Western Diamondback Rattlesnake and the Timber Rattlesnake, the potency of the venom appears to be higher in newborns than in adults. The fangs are of moderate length, ranging from 0.28" to 0.35" (7–9 mm) in adults.

Remarks: Natural longevities are unknown; a captive

individual lived in excess of 19 years. There is some suggestion that gopher snakes mimic this species to some degree, since elsewhere, where their ranges overlap, they share aspects of color, pattern and behavior. The precise nature of this relationship, if any, in Texas remains to be studied.

Massasauga

Scientific Name: *Sistrurus catenatus* (Rafinesque, 1818). The Latin name *catenatus* means "chained" or "chain-like," in reference to the dorsal pattern. (The common name, Massasauga, means "great river-mouth" in the Native American Ojibwa language, probably in reference to the marshy habitat of this snake in the region of the Great Lakes).

Subspecies: Three subspecies are recognized; two of these, the Desert Massasauga *(S. c. edwardsii)* and the Western Massasauga *(S. c. tergeminus)*, occur in Texas. The Latin name *tergeminus* means "threefold" or "triple," in reference to the three rows of prominent dorsolateral blotches in this form. The Latin name *edwardsii* is a patronym honoring L.A. Edwards, a U.S. Army surgeon who collected the type-specimen on one of the mid-nineteenth-century exploring expeditions of the American West sponsored by the U.S. government.

Description: Massasaugas are small rattlesnakes; adults are typically 18–26" (450–650 mm) in length. The largest recorded specimens are 35" (883 mm) for *tergeminus* and 21" (530 mm) for *edwardsii*. There are 21–27 (usually 23 or 25) scale rows at midbody, and all but one or two of these are keeled. Males possess between 129 and 155 ventral and between 24 and 36 subcaudal scales; corresponding counts in females range from 132 to 160 and from 19 to 29, respectively. Up to nine distal subcaudals may be divided. The top of the head bears the nine enlarged plates characteristic of

Desert Massasauga *(Sistrurus catenatus edwardsii)*

the genus (see p. 51).

This is a light-gray-to-grayish-brown snake with 27–50 grayish-brown mid-dorsal blotches, bordered with dark brown or black and narrowly outlined with white. Two or three lateral series of similar but smaller blotches occur on each side. The lateral and mid-dorsal blotches are rarely in contact; the lowest lateral series may extend onto the ventral scales, which range from heavily spotted with dark pigment to immaculate (i.e., without spots). There are 3–11 brown crossbands on the tail. A transverse brown bar crosses the head in front of the eyes. A variable dark brown

Western Massasauga (*Sistrurus catenatus tergeminus*)

marking, often lyre-shaped, extends backward on top of the head. A white-edged dark brown stripe 2–3 scales wide extends backward to the angle of the mouth and beyond; this white edge extends forward on the face to the opening of the pit organ. The tail is short and the rattle small. Newborn young have yellow tails; these assume typical coloration by the following year.

Similar Species: The Pygmy Rattlesnake is smaller and lighter in color, has a mid-dorsal light orange or orange-brown stripe, and the upper preocular scales are separated from the postnasal scale by a large loreal scale. All other

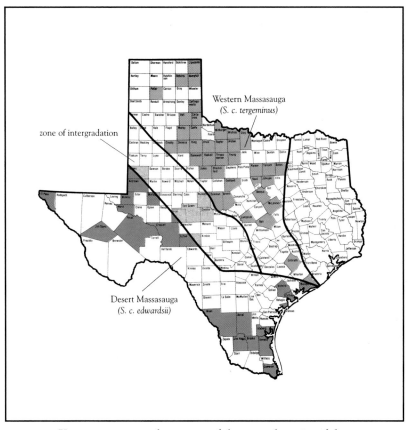

zone of intergradation

Western Massasauga
(*S. c. terginus*)

Desert Massasauga
(*S. c. edwardsii*)

Known occurrence, by county, of the two subspecies of the Massasauga *(Sistrurus catenatus)*

species of rattlesnake native to Texas have many smaller scales, rather than the nine large plates characteristic of the Massasauga, on top of the head. Hognose snakes (genus *Heterodon*), which are nonvenomous, lack any semblance of a rattle or the facial pit characteristic of rattlesnakes, and have a distinctly upturned rostral scale.

Habitat: This is a characteristic inhabitant of tall-grass prairies in central Texas, such as the Grand Prairie southwest of Fort Worth and at Waco, as well as short-grass prairies and open thornscrub elsewhere in the state. Seasonal wetlands are often important features of occupied habitat. Massasaugas tend to hibernate in wetter areas, and move to drier and/or upland habitats during the summer.

Behavior: This species is nocturnal or crepuscular (see glossary) during the hot summer months but diurnal during spring and fall. It can be found from March through October, and is most active from April to early June in north-central Texas and from July to August in the Panhandle. This may reflect the tendency of individual snakes to move farther and more often during the summer than at other times of the activity season. This species may be abundant in a given area, but individuals may seldom be seen because they are cryptic (see glossary). Massasaugas are good swimmers and readily enter water. They are relatively sedentary snakes, moving on average about 33 feet (10 meters) per day, and occupying a home range of less than 11,960 square yards (10,000 m²). Gravid females (see glossary) occupy smaller areas than other adults.

Reproduction: Little is known about reproduction in Texas populations. Courtship behavior resembles that seen in the Western Diamondback Rattlesnake, although it is not as prolonged. Females attain sexual maturity at about 15.75" (400 mm) in length, perhaps in their third year. Litter size ranges from 3 to 11. Individual females may exhibit parental care, remaining with the newborn young until their first shed.

Food Habits: Massasaugas are opportunistic predators and take a wide variety of vertebrate prey, as well as invertebrates. Known food items in Texas include leopard frogs, lizards (whiptails, skinks and spiny lizards), snakes (ground snakes and lined snakes), short-tailed shrews, pocket mice and harvest mice.

Venom Characteristics: Venom yields from adults are small, averaging 14 mg (dry weight), with a maximum of 37 mg. LD_{50} values of 0.2–0.9 mg/kg (i.p.) and 5.25–6.8 mg/kg (s.c.) have been reported. The lethal human dose is unknown and undoubtedly variable, but has been estimated at 30–40 mg; human fatalities from this species are rare, and none have been reported in Texas. The fangs are relatively short, ranging from 0.16" to 0.24" (4–6 mm) in adults.

Remarks: Modification and/or destruction of its native grassland habitats may be eliminating this species from areas throughout its range, although such long-term, widespread trends are hard to pin down with accurate data. The species is certainly becoming less abundant in many areas. Natural longevity is unknown, but captive individuals have lived more than 12 years *(S. c. edwardsii)* and more than 20 years *(S. c. tergeminus)*.

Pygmy Rattlesnake

Scientific Name: *Sistrurus miliarius* (Linnaeus, 1766). The Latin name *miliarius* means "millet" or "millet-like," presumably in reference to the blotched dorsal pattern.

Subspecies: Three subspecies are recognized; of these, the Western Pygmy Rattlesnake *(S. m. streckeri)* occurs in Texas. This subspecies is named in honor of Texas' pioneering herpetologist in the early twentieth century, Dr. John K. Strecker of Baylor University.

Description: Pygmies are small rattlesnakes; adults are 1–1.5' (300–500 mm) in length. The largest recorded specimen was a male measuring 25" (638 mm) in length, although the specimen was in captivity, so growth was probably artificially enhanced. The tail is slender and the rattle tiny. There are 21 (occasionally 23) dorsal scale rows, all keeled, at midbody. Ventral scales number between 123 and 135, and average 127 in males and 129 in females. Subcaudals number between 27 and 38 in males and between 27 and 34 in females, the distal 1–11 (see glossary) often divided. There are nine large plates, characteristic of the genus, on top of the head. The loreal scale is relatively large, in broad contact with the prefrontal scale, and separating the preoc-

Western Pygmy Rattlesnake *(Sistrurus miliarius streckeri)*

ular scales from the postnasal ones.

The dorsal ground color is pale grayish-brown, with light stippling of darker brown. A median dorsal series of 23–42 dark brown blotches, conspicuously wider than they are long and irregularly bordered with white, extends from the neck to the tail. An additional 1 or 2 lateral series of blotches may occur on each side. Irregular brown blotches occur on the snout, and a wide light bar crosses the head behind them. A pair of undulating brown stripes, sometimes forming a lyre-shaped pattern, extends from the bar to the neck.

A dark brown cheek stripe extends posteriorly from each eye to the angle of the mouth. A reddish-brown mid-dorsal stripe extends from the back of the head to the base of the tail. Dorsal bands, more or less transverse and 7–14 in number, occur on the tail itself. The tails of newborns are sulphur-yellow in color, fading with age.

Similar Species: Massasaugas are larger and darker, and the upper preocular scales are in contact with the postnasal scale. All other rattlesnake species native to Texas have many smaller scales, rather than nine large plates, on top of the head. Hognose snakes (genus *Heterodon*), which are nonvenomous, lack any semblance of a rattle or the facial pit characteristic of rattlesnakes, and have a distinctly upturned rostral scale.

Habitat: Individuals are frequently found beneath decaying logs, pieces of bark, palmetto fronds and other organic debris in open upland loblolly pine/hardwood forests, bottomland hardwoods, mesic grasslands of eastern Texas, and the open agricultural lands, rice fields and bar ditches along the upper Coastal Plain.

Behavior: Very little is known about the behavior of this species in the wild. It is probably an ambush predator, since individuals are highly cryptic and spend most of their time hidden. The sound of the tiny rattle is barely audible and easily mistaken for a cicada or other insect. When disturbed, these snakes may bob their heads vertically in addition to rattling. Individuals may be surface-active throughout the year at body temperatures of 59°–99°F (15°–37°C), particularly when water-table levels are high.

Reproduction: Pygmy rattlesnakes in Texas probably mate in the fall, like their Florida counterparts. Females are gravid in the spring and give birth in July and August. Most females from a Florida population that has been studied were not gravid in consecutive years. Average litter size is about 6, with a normal range of 2–11. Larger females give

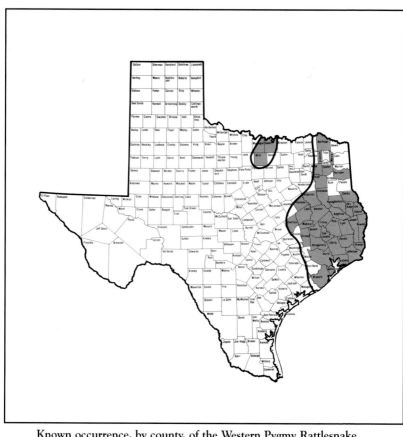

Known occurrence, by county, of the Western Pygmy Rattlesnake
(Sistrurus miliarius streckeri)

birth to larger litters; one large female produced a litter of 32 young. Newborn snakes weigh 0.07–0.21 ounces (2–6 gm) and are about 4–8" (110–200 mm) in length. Females may remain with newborns until the latter shed their skins for the first time. Males engage in physical combat (the so-called "combat dance") to establish social dominance, which probably facilitates access to females. Male combat rituals are not as energetic as they are in other pitviper species.

Food Habits: A variety of prey items are taken, including insects, centipedes, frogs and toads, lizards, small snakes, nestling birds and small mammals. Juvenile and young snakes may utilize their brightly colored tail tips as lures to attract prey to within striking distance.

Venom Characteristics: Data are very limited and exist only for the eastern subspecies. Venom yields from adults are small, ranging from 18 to 34 mg (dry weight). LD_{50} values of 2.8–12.6 mg/kg (i.v.), 6.0–7.0 mg/kg (i.p.) and 24.25 mg/kg (s.c.) have been reported. The fangs are relatively short, ranging from 0.2" to 0.24" (5–6 mm) in adults. This species is not believed to be capable of inflicting a fatal bite on a person because of its small size and weak venom, and no fatalities are known from the bite of this species.

Remarks: Natural longevity for this subspecies is unknown, although a captive individual lived more than 16 years.

THE ELAPIDAE

This is a relatively recent family of venomous snakes that appeared abruptly in the fossil record of the Old World about 25 million years ago during the Miocene epoch. Members apparently dispersed into North America across the Bering Land Bridge shortly thereafter. Today there are more than 270 species distributed among 62 genera worldwide, with the greatest centers of diversity in Africa, Southeast Asia and Australia. The group includes such familiar snakes as cobras, kraits, mambas, tiger snakes, seasnakes and coral snakes. Most species lay eggs but some, notably the seasnakes, give birth to live young. All are characterized by having a relatively short and permanently erect fang on each maxilla at the front of the mouth (*proteroglyphy*). There are replacement fangs located behind the functional one to replace it when necessary. Elapids lack the lever-and-pulley fang mechanism of vipers and pitvipers, and their fangs fit into grooved slots in the floor of the mouth when the mouth is closed.

The venom gland in coral snakes is located on each side of the upper jaw behind the eye, and is connected by a duct to an open sinus at the base of each fang. The duct is surrounded by a simple mucus gland with many tiny tubules emptying into it, and the entire system is covered by a tough connective tissue capsule protecting it from injury. Venom is forced from the gland by the contraction of muscles located above and behind it, and is delivered from the fang sinus into the wound by means of the chewing motions characteristic of coral snakes. Small quantities of venom are also secreted from infralabial glands located in the lower jaw.

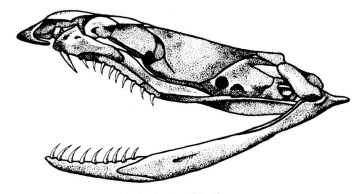

Skull of a Coral Snake
Side view showing one of the two short, fixed fangs at the front of the upper jaw. Note smaller teeth which almost always contribute to the bite pattern.

Harlequin Coral Snake

Scientific Name: *Micrurus fulvius* (Linnaeus, 1766). The generic name means "small tail" in Latin and the species name *fulvius* means "orange" or "orange-yellow," apparently in reference to the faded red bands of the first preserved specimen(s) seen by Linnaeus.

Subspecies: Five subspecies are recognized; of these, one, the Texas Coral Snake (*M. f. tener*), occurs in Texas. The Latin name *tener* means "tender" or "delicate," in reference to the slender build of this form.

Description: Texas Coral Snakes are slender and medium-sized, with a head not discernibly larger than the body.

Adults are typically 15–25" (380–635 mm) in length, with the largest recorded specimen for this subspecies, from Brazoria County, Texas, measuring 3'11.75" (1,213 mm) in length. Females are, on average, larger than males. There are 15 smooth scale rows at midbody. The anal plate is divided. There are 200–211 ventral scales and 38–46 subcaudal scales in males, and 219–227 and 26–34, respectively, in females. The nose is black, and males have 10–14 black body bands, while females have 15. The red body bands are often speckled with irregular black dots which have a tendency to be concentrated toward the scale tips. The yellow bands are immaculate (i.e., without spots) and 1–2 scales wide. The color bands continue onto the ventral surface.

Similar Species: In Texas, the old adage "red touch yellow, kill a fellow; red touch black, venom lack" still serves to distinguish this venomous species from other brightly banded species of snakes, all of which are harmless. None of these other species, such as milksnakes (*Lampropeltis triangulum*) and scarlet snakes (*Cemophora coccinea*), have red and yellow (or whitish) bands touching each other. This adage does not work, however, in the New World tropics, where the greatest diversity of coral-snake species and their mimics occur.

Habitat: The Texas Coral Snake inhabits a wide variety of terrestrial situations, including urban and suburban ones, from east Texas pine forests to oak-juniper canyons along the Pecos River, provided sufficient rock-crevice cover or thick plant litter exists. These snakes can be very abundant but never seen because of their habits.

Behavior: Coral Snakes spend most of their time underground (*fossoriality*) or sheltering under suitable objects, but can be active on the surface during the day in early spring or at other times when rainfall has saturated the ground. They appear not to be generally surface-active at night. Males are most active in the late fall or early spring, when

Texas Coral Snake *(Micrurus fulvius tener)*

they are searching for mates, and females are most active in late summer and throughout the fall, when they are searching for prey to build energy reserves for the next season's reproductive effort. Coral snakes will attempt to escape if discovered and individuals may engage in complex defensive behavior if prevented from doing so. Such behavior includes hiding the head beneath body coils, mimicking the head with the tail (including crawling backward and striking with the tail), erratic body movements and feigning death. Other individuals can be temperamental and readily bite if in any way restrained.

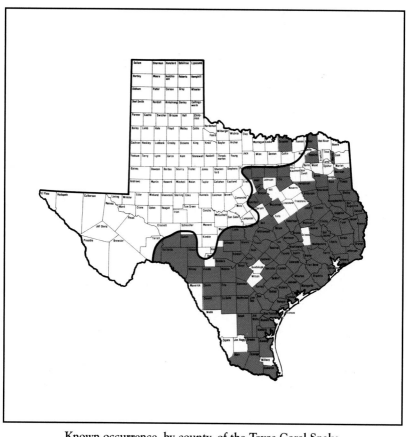

Known occurrence, by county, of the Texas Coral Snake
(Micrurus fulvius tener)

Reproduction: Males attain sexual maturity at an age of 12–21 months and at a length of about 16" (400 mm), and females do so at 15 months of age and about 20" (500 mm) in length. Mating takes place from October through May, and a clutch of 2–13 eggs is laid in May or June. Common nesting sites include rotten logs, under rocks, and underground. Eggs hatch from the end of August into October, and hatchlings are about 8" (200 mm) long.

Food Habits: Texas Coral Snakes eat other snakes (*ophiophagy*), including occasionally each other, as well as elongate lizards such as skinks and glass lizards. Snakes eaten are primarily fossorial or semi-fossorial, such as worm snakes, ringneck snakes, brown snakes, blackhead snakes and earth snakes, but the young of many other snake species, including copperheads and cottonmouths, are occasionally consumed. Coral snakes are active foragers, on the move in search of prey items which they may recognize through chemical and/or visual cues. Prey species are grasped and held while chewing movements are employed to work venom into the victim. The prey is quickly immobilized by the powerful venom, and usually swallowed head-first. In turn, coral snakes fall prey to other predators as diverse as bullfrogs and opossums, and most notably to birds such as hawks and shrikes.

Venom Characteristics: Coral-snake venom is a complex array of proteins, mostly enzymes and other polypeptides, along with nonprotein substances such as riboflavin and metallic salts (zinc, calcium, magnesium and potassium) which act synergistically to produce lethal effects. Coral-snake venom produces very little local tissue damage, hemorrhaging or swelling. Lethal effects from Texas Coral Snake venom may occur in two ways: (1) venom blocks the junctions between and interferes with chemical communication between nerves and muscles, causing death by suffocation when muscles of the respiratory system are paralyzed; and (2) venom acts directly on the heart and cardiovascular system, causing a marked decrease in heart rate and blood pressure and death from shock. The venom yield for this subspecies is 2–28 mg dry weight, and is positively correlated with body size. Published LD_{50} values include 0.97 mg/kg (i.p.), 0.28 mg/kg (i.v.) and 2.60 mg/kg (s.c.). The lethal human dose is unknown and undoubtedly variable, but has been estimated at 4–7 mg/kg. Coral snakes apparently possess no immunity to their own venom.

Human envenomations are relatively uncommon (comprising from 20-40% of reported bites), partly because of the coral snake's primitive delivery mechanism, its small size and its generally inoffensive nature. In a definitive study of coral-snake bites published in 1987, 34 of 39 patients (87%) were bitten either on a finger or thumb or on the thin skin fold between the index finger and thumb. Of the thirty-two victims for whom information was available, only eight suffered "legitimate" bites. Twenty-three others were deliberately handling the snake (fourteen through misidentification), and eight of these were inebriated. Human fatalities are now entirely preventable with antivenom treatment coupled with appropriate surgical intervention (see Snakebite section, p. 21).

Remarks: A debate between scientists has existed for over a century about whether the bright coloration of coral snakes is aposematic (i.e., serves to warn potential predators of their deadly nature), and about whether similarly colored nonpoisonous species of snakes derive enhanced protection from potential predators by mimicking the pattern and behavior of coral snakes. Studies in the field suggest strongly that both situations are true, and this is supported by experimental evidence with potential avian predators. However, recent experiments with mammals have produced contrary results, suggesting that more work needs to be done to understand the function of bright colors in snakes. The ringed pattern of coral snakes may also serve a disruptive function in their natural habitats, concealing and breaking up the body outline and thus making it more difficult for potential predators to aim an effective attack.

Natural longevities for this species are unknown, but a captive individual lived in excess of 18 years, a notable accomplishment in itself, as this species is very difficult to maintain in captivity.

Useful Sources of Information

There is a central hotline for the Texas Poison Center; the number is **1-800-764-7661**. *Calling this number will route you to the regional center closest to you, or to the next available one if the first number is busy. Or you may contact a regional center directly with the information given below:*

South Texas Poison Center
University of Texas Health Science
   Center at San Antonio
Room 146, Forensic Science Building
7703 Floyd Curl Drive
San Antonio, TX 78284-7849
210-567-5762

Central Texas Poison Center
Scott and White Memorial Hospital
2401 South 31st St.
Temple, TX 76508
817-724-7403

North Texas Poison Center
P.O. Box 35926
5201 Harry Hines Boulevard
Dallas, TX 75235
214-589-0911

Southeast Texas Poison Center
Clinical Pharmacology and
   Toxicology Unit
The University of Texas Medical Branch
301 University Boulevard
Galveston, TX 77555-1031
409-772-9612 or 766-4403

West Texas Regional
   Poison Center
4800 Alameda Avenue
El Paso, TX 79905
915-534-3800

Panhandle Poison Center
1501 South Coulter
Amarillo, TX 79106
806-354-1630

Arizona Poison and
   Drug Information Center
University of Arizona
1501 N. Campbell Avenue
Tucson, AZ 85724
520-626-6016

Therapeutic Antibodies, Inc.
1207 17th Avenue South,
#103
Nashville, TN 37212
615-327-1027

Wyeth-Ayerst Laboratories, Inc..
P.O. Box 8299
Philadelphia, PA 19101
717-426-1941

Glossary

anaphylaxis: hypersensitivity to a foreign substance resulting in a severe or fatal systemic breakdown characterized by respiratory distress, fainting, itching and skin rashes

anticoagulant: a substance which prevents blood from clotting

apical: of or pertaining to the posterior tip of the dorsal scales

arthropod: any member of the phylum Arthropoda, a major grouping characterized by segmented bodies and jointed legs, and including insects, arachnids and crustaceans

bajada: "down below" (Spanish); a name given to an alluvial outwash slope extending from the mouth of a canyon downward to an intermountain basin in many parts of the desert southwest

congener: a species or subspecies that is a member of the same genus as the species or subspecies under discussion

conspecific: an individual organism that is a member of the same species as the individual under discussion

crepuscular: active primarily at twilight and/or dawn

crypsis: the ability of an organism to escape detection through a combination of behavior and camouflage ("Cryptic" is the adjective)

cyanosis: bluish-black discoloration around the bite area resulting from significant local tissue breakdown

dalton: an atomic mass unit equal to 1/12 of the mass of an atom of C^{12}; approximately 16598×10^{-24} grams

defibrination: the condition in which plasma fibrinogen, an important component of the blood-clotting mechanism, is absent

distal: more distant from a point of origin; in the case of the scales under the tail, those further away from the vent

dorsal: of or pertaining to the upper surface of the body

ecchymosis: severe discoloration of the skin resulting from the leakage of blood from ruptured blood vessels into surrounding tissue

fasciculations: small, local involuntary muscular contractions visible under the skin, most noticeable in the area of the bite, as well as on the face and over the large muscle groups of the back and neck, representing spontaneous discharge of motor neurons from the action of several venom components

5'-nucleotidase: an enzyme which specifically acts to cleave the bond between the 5' end of a nucleotide and its phosphate group; the net result is destruction of the functional integrity of a DNA or RNA molecule

genera: plural of genus, the category just above the species level in the Linnean taxonomic hierarchy

glycosuria: the presence of excess glucose in the urine

gravid: pregnant or containing a mass of enlarged eggs almost ready to be laid

hematemesis: vomiting of blood

hematuria: the discharge of blood in the urine

hemolytic: causing the destruction or dissolution of red blood cells

hemorrhagic: causing the extensive destruction of cells forming the lining of blood vessels

hibernacula: plural of hibernaculum; any place where an animal seeks shelter when entering into a state of decreased physiological activity during the winter

hyaluronidase: an enzyme that hydrolyzes hyaluronic acid, causing connective tissue to dissociate, thus losing its functional integrity and allowing venom components to reach other target tissues and organ systems more quickly; also called "spreading factor"

hypotensive: of or pertaining to low blood pressure

immunoassay: the identification of a substance such as a protein through its ability to provoke an immune response

infralabial: below the lower line of the mouth

intersupraocular scale: a scale on top of the head lying between the supraocular scales

i.p.: intraperitoneal; refers to injection of a substance into the body cavity of a vertebrate animal

isoform: one of several three-dimensional configurations that a specific molecule may take

i.v.: intravenous; refers to injection of a substance into the circulatory system of a vertebrate animal

keeled: pertaining to scales with an elevated, longitudinal ridge which may or may not extend from base to tip, and which are either sharp and well-defined or broad and obtuse

LD_{50}: the venom dosage, expressed as milligrams of venom per kilogram of the test animal (usually mice), which is lethal to 50% of the experimental subjects during a 24-hour period in a clinical trial

lethal dose: see LD_{50} (above)

loreal scale: the scales on either side of the head located between the preocular scales and the postnasal scale

lyre: a stringed musical instrument similar in shape to a harp; used in reference to dorsal head markings on some snakes which suggest the shape of this instrument

melena: the presence of blood in the stools

myolytic: causing the disintegration or liquification of muscle tissue

necrosis: tissue death; can be followed by gangrene and necessitate amputation if left untreated; largely preventable with appropriate antivenom therapy

neurotoxin: a toxin which primarily or exclusively affects the nervous system

parietal scale: a scale lying on top of the head behind the supraocular scales

peptide: a subunit of a protein consisting of multiple amino acids joined together by amide bonds

phospholipase: an enzyme which hydrolyzes phospholipids, which are major components of biological membranes

postocular: behind the eye

prefoveal scale: one of the small scales surrounding the opening of the infrared receptor on each side of the face of pitvipers

preocular scale: the scale located directly in front of the eye

protease: a general class of enzymes which break up proteins into smaller subunits

proteinuria: the presence of excess serum protein in the urine

proteolytic: causing the destruction or dissociation of proteins through the hydrolysis of peptide bonds

rhomboid: a four-sided shape, each side equal in length, with the diagonally opposite angles equal to each other, and in which two angles are acute and two are obtuse

rostral scale: the scale forming the tip of the snout

s.c.: subcutaneous; refers to injection of a substance beneath the surface skin layers but not directly into the circulatory system or body cavity of a vertebrate animal

scale row: a longitudinal series of dorsal or lateral scales

sexual dimorphism: the condition of diagnostic morphological differences existing between the sexes within a species

subcaudal scales: the scales that cover the underside of the tail

supraocular scale: the large plate that lies above the eye

symphyses: plural of symphysis, a cartilaginous joint between two bones

talus: an accumulation of rock fragments below steep slopes or cliffs

transverse: perpendicular to the long axis of the body

undulating: furnished with wave-like markings

ventral: of or pertaining to the lower surface of the body

vesiculations: swellings of the skin filled with clear serous fluid or blood; they usually occur in the vicinity of the bite, but can involve the entire extremity in serious cases

Selected Bibliography

General References:

Boundy, J. 1995. Maximum lengths of North American snakes. *Bull. Chicago Herpetol. Soc.* 30(6):109-122.

Campbell, J.A. and E.D. Brodie, Jr. (eds.). 1992. *Biology of the Pitvipers.* Selva, Tyler, Texas. xi + 467 p.

Campbell, J.A. and W.W. Lamar. 1989. *The Venomous Reptiles of Latin America.* Cornell Univ. Press, Ithaca, New York. xii + 425 p.

Carpenter, C.C. and J.C. Gillingham. 1975. Postural responses to kingsnakes by crotaline snakes. *Herpetologica* 31(3):293-302.

Chiszar, D., C.W. Radcliffe, and H.M. Smith. 1978. Chemosensory searching for wounded prey by rattlesnakes is released by striking: a replication report. *Herpetol. Rev.* 9(2):54-56.

Cook, P.M., M.P. Rowe, and R.W. Van Devender. 1994. Allometric scaling and interspecific differences in the rattling sounds of rattlesnakes. *Herpetologica* 50(3):358-368.

Dixon, J.R. 1987. *Amphibians and Reptiles of Texas, with Keys, Taxonomic Synopses, Bibliography, and Distribution Maps.* Texas A&M Univ. Press, College Station. xii + 434 p.

Dobie, J.F. 1965. *Rattlesnakes.* Little, Brown and Co., New York. 201 p.

Ernst, C.H. 1992. *Venomous Reptiles of North America.* Smithsonian Inst. Press, Washington, D.C. ix + 236 p.

Ernst, C.H. and G.R. Zug. 1996. *Snakes in Question.* Smithsonian Inst. Press, Washington, D.C. xvii + 203 p.

Estes, R., K. de Queiroz, and J. Gauthier. 1988. Phylogenetic relationships within Squamata, p. 119-281. In R. Estes and G. Pregill (eds.), *Phylogenetic Relationships of the Lizard Families: Essays commemorating Charles L. Camp.* Stanford Univ. Press, Stanford, California. xii + 631 p.

Fenton, M.B. and L.E. Licht. 1990. Why rattle snake? *J. Herpetol.* 24(3):274-279.

Forstner, M.R.J., S.K. Davis, and E. Arevalo. 1995. Support for the hypothesis of anguimorph ancestry for the suborder Serpentes from phylogenetic analysis of mitochondrial DNA sequences. *Mol. Phylo. Evol.* 4(1):93-102.

Gans, C. 1961. The feeding mechanism of snakes and its possible evolution. *Amer. Zool.* 1(2):217-227.

Gloyd, H.K. and R. Conant. 1990. *Snakes of the Agkistrodon Complex: A*

Monographic Review. Soc. Study Amphib. Rept., Oxford, Ohio. vi + 614 p.

Greene, H.L. 1997. *Snakes: the Evolution of Mystery in Nature.* Univ. California Press, Berkeley. 365 p.

Hartline, P.H., L. Kass, and M.S. Loop. 1978. Merging of modalities in the optic tectum: infrared and visual integration in rattlesnakes. *Science* 199:1225-1229.

Klauber, L.M. 1972. *Rattlesnakes: Their Habits, Life Histories, and Influence on Mankind.* Vol. I, xxx + 1-740 pp., Vol. II, xvii + 741-1533 pp. Univ. California Press, Berkeley.

Kraus, F., D.G. Mink, and W.M. Brown. 1996. Crotaline intergeneric relationships based on mitochondrial DNA sequence data. *Copeia* 1996(4):763-773.

Lee, M.S.Y. 1997. The phylogeny of varanoid lizards and the affinities of snakes. *Philos. Trans. R. Soc. Lond.* B 352:53-91.

Minton, S.A., Jr. and M.R. Minton. 1969. *Venomous Reptiles.* Charles Scribner's Sons, New York. xii + 274 p.

Schaeffer, P.J., K.E. Conley, and S.L. Lindstedt. 1996. Structural correlates of speed and endurance in skeletal muscle: the rattlesnake tailshaker muscle. *J. Exp. Biol.* 199:351-358.

Schmidt, K.P. 1945. The girl who had never been bitten by a rattlesnake: a Texas folktale. *Chicago Nat.* 8(2):30-31.

Schwenk, K. 1994. Why snakes have forked tongues. *Science* 263:1573-1577.

Schwenk, K. 1995. The serpent's tongue. *Nat. Hist.* 104(4):48-54.

Seigel, R.A. and J.T. Collins (eds.). 1993. *Snakes: Ecology and Behavior.* McGraw-Hill, Inc., New York. xvi + 414 p.

Seigel, R.A., J.T. Collins, and S.S. Novak (eds.). 1987. *Snakes: Ecology and Evolutionary Biology.* Macmillan Publ. Co., New York. xiv + 529 p.

Shaw, C.E. and S. Campbell. 1974. *Snakes of the American West.* Alfred A. Knopf, New York. xii + 330 p.

Tennant, A. 1984. *The Snakes of Texas.* Texas Monthly Press, Austin. 561 p.

Thorpe, R.S., W. Wüster, and A. Malhotra (eds.). 1997. *Venomous Snakes: Ecology, Evolution and Snakebite.* Oxford Univ. Press, New York. xix + 276 p.

Yaron, Z. 1985. Reptilian placentation and gestation: structure, function, and endocrine control, p. 527-603. *In* C. Gans and F. Billett (eds.), *Biology of the Reptilia.* Vol. 15. Development B. John Wiley and Sons, New York. x + 731 p.

Venoms and Snakebite:

Burgess, J.L. and R.C. Dart. 1991. Snake venom coagulopathy: use and abuse of blood products in the treatment of pit viper envenomation. *Ann. Emerg. Med.* 20:795-801.

Burgess, J.L., R.C. Dart, N.B. Egen, and M. Mayersohn. 1992. Effects of constriction bands on rattlesnake venom absorption: a pharmacokinetic study. *Ann. Emerg. Med.* 21:1086-1093.

Gans, C. and K.A. Gans (eds.). 1978. *Biology of the Reptilia.* Vol. 8. Physiology B. Academic Press, New York. xiii + 782 p.

Glass, T.G., Jr., M.D., F.A.C.S. 1976. *Management of Poisonous Snakebite.* Privately printed, San Antonio, Texas. 182 pp., unnum.

Glenn, J.L. and R.C. Straight. 1982. The rattlesnakes and their venom yield and lethal toxicity, p. 3-119. *in* A.T. Tu (ed.), *Rattlesnake Venoms, Their Actions and Treatment.* Marcel Dekker, New York.

Hardy, D.L., Sr. 1994. Snakebite and field biologists in Mexico and Central America: report on ten cases with recommendations for field management. *Herpetol. Nat. Hist.* 2(2):67-82.

Hayes, W.K., P. Lavin-Murcio, and K.V. Kardong. 1995. Northern Pacific Rattlesnakes *(Crotalus viridis oreganus)* meter venom when feeding on prey of different sizes. *Copeia* 1995(2):337-343.

Kardong, K.V. 1996. Snake toxins and venoms: an evolutionary perspective. *Herpetologica* 52(1):36-46.

Minton, S.A. 1987. Poisonous snakes and snakebite in the U.S.: a brief review. *Northwest Sci.* 61(2):130-137.

Parrish, H.M., J.C. Goldner, and S.I. Silberg. 1966. Poisonous snakebites causing no venenation. *Postgrad. Med.* 39(3):265-269.

Pope, C.H. and R.M. Perkins. 1944. Differences in the patterns of bites of venomous and harmless snakes. *Arch. Surg.* 49: 331-336.

Russell, F.E. 1980. Snake venom poisoning in the United States. *Ann. Rev. Med.* 31:247-259.

Russell, F.E. 1983. *Snake venom poisoning.* Scholium Intl., Inc., Great Neck, New York. xiv + 562 p.

Soto, J.G., J.C. Perez, M.M. Lopez, M. Martinez, T.B. Quintanilla-Hernandez, M.S. Santa-Hernandez, K. Turner, J.L. Glenn, R.C. Straight, and S.A. Minton. 1989. Comparative enzymatic study of HPLC-fractionated *Crotalus* venoms. *Comp. Biochem. Physiol.* 93B(4):847-855

Tan, N.-H. and G. Ponnudurai. 1990. A comparative study of the biological activities of venoms from snakes of the genus *Agkistrodon* (moccasins and copperheads). *Comp.Biochem. Physiol.* 95B(3):577-582.

Tan, N.-H. and G. Ponnudurai. 1991. A comparative study of the biological activities of rattlesnake (genera *Crotalus* and *Sistrurus*) venoms. *Comp. Biochem. Physiol.* 98C(2/3):455-461.

Thomas, R.G. and F.H. Pough. 1979. The effect of rattlesnake venom on digestion of prey. *Toxicon* 17(3):221-228.

Tu, A.T. 1982. Chemistry of rattlesnake venoms, p. 247-312. *in* A.T. Tu (ed.), *Rattlesnake Venoms, Their Actions and Treatment.* Marcel Dekker, New York.

Van Mierop, L.H.S. 1976. Poisonous snakebite: a review, 2. Symptomology and treatment. *J. Florida Med. Asso.* 63:201-209.

Weinstein, S.A., C.F. DeWitt, and L.A. Smith. 1992. Variability of venom-neutralizing properties of serum from snakes of the colubrid genus *Lampropeltis. J. Herpetol.* 26(4):452-461.

Wingert, W.A. and J. Wainschel. 1975. Diagnosis and management of envenomation by poisonous snakes. *South. Med. J.* 68(8):1015-1026.

Copperhead:

Fitch, H.S. 1960. Autecology of the Copperhead. *Univ. Kansas Publ. Mus. Nat. Hist.* 13(4):85-288.

Ford, N.B., V.A. Cobb, and W.W. Lamar. 1990. Reproductive data on snakes from northeastern Texas. *Texas J. Sci.* 42(4):355-368.

Lagesse, L.A. and N.B. Ford. 1996. Ontogenetic variation in the diet of the Southern Copperhead, *Agkistrodon contortrix*, in northeastern Texas. *Texas J. Sci.* 48(1):48-54.

Moran, J.B. and C.R. Geren. 1980. Subspecific variations in *Agkistrodon contortrix* venoms—II. *Comp. Biochem. Physiol.* 65B(4):739-742.

Sanders, J.S. and J.S. Jacob. 1981. Thermal ecology of the Copperhead (*Agkistrodon contortrix*). *Herpetologica* 37(4):264-270.

Schuett, G.W. and D. Duvall. 1996. Head lifting by female Copperheads, *Agkistrodon contortrix*, during courtship: potential mate choice. *Anim. Behav.* 51(2):367-373.

Schuett, G.W. and J.C. Gillingham. 1986. Sperm storage and multiple paternity in the Copperhead, *Agkistrodon contortrix. Copeia* 1986(3):807-811.

Seifert, W. 1972. Amphibians and reptiles in Texas Part two: habitat, variations & intergradations of the Trans Pecos Copperhead *Agkistrodon contortrix pictigaster* in Texas. *Bull. Dallas Mus. Nat. Hist.* (2):1-10.

Stewart, B.G. 1984. Life history notes. *Agkistrodon contortrix laticinctus* (Broad-banded Copperhead). Combat. *Herpetol. Rev.* 15(1):17.

Vial, J.L., T.L. Berger, and W.T. McWilliams, Jr. 1977. Quantitative demography of copperheads, *Agkistrodon contortrix* (Serpentes: Viperidae). *Res. Pop. Ecol.* 18(2):223-234.

Cottonmouth:

Burkett, R.D. 1966. Natural history of Cottonmouth Moccasin, *Agkistrodon piscivorus* (Reptilia). *Univ. Kansas Publ. Mus. Nat. Hist.* 17(9):435-491.

Cottam, C., W.C. Glazener, and G.G. Raun. 1959. Notes on food of moccasins and rattlesnakes from the Welder Wildlife Refuge, Sinton, Texas. *Contrib. Welder Wildl. Found.* (45):1-9.

Wharton, C.H. 1960. Birth and behavior of a brood of cottonmouths, *Agkistrodon piscivorus piscivorus* with notes on tail-luring. *Herpetologica* 16(2):125-129.

Wharton, C.H. 1966. Reproduction and growth in the cottonmouths, *Agkistrodon piscivorus* Lácèpede, of Cedar Keys, Florida. *Copeia* 1966(2):149-161.

Wharton, C.H. 1969. The Cottonmouth Moccasin on Sea Horse Key, Florida. *Bull. Florida St. Mus.* 14(3):227-272.

Western Diamondback Rattlesnake:

Beavers, R.A. 1976. Food habits of the Western Diamondback Rattlesnake, *Crotalus atrox*, in Texas (Viperidae). *Southwest. Nat.* 20(4):503-515.

Fitch, H.S. and G.R. Pisani. 1993. Life history traits of the Western Diamondback Rattlesnake *(Crotalus atrox)* studied from roundup samples in Oklahoma. *Occ. Pap. Mus. Nat. Hist. Univ. Kansas* (156): 1-24.

Gillingham, J.C. and R.E. Baker. 1981. Evidence for scavenging behavior in the Western Diamondback Rattlesnake *(Crotalus atrox)*. *Z. Tierpsychol.* 55(3):217-227.

Gillingham, J.C., C.C. Carpenter, and J.B. Murphy. 1983. Courtship, male combat and dominance in the Western Diamondback Rattlesnake, *Crotalus atrox. J. Herpetol.* 17(3):265-270.

Gillingham, J.C. and D.L. Clark. 1981. An analysis of prey searching behavior in the Western Diamondback Rattlesnake, *Crotalus atrox. Behav. Neural. Biol.* 32:235-240.

Gloyd, H.K. 1948. Another account of the "dance" of the Western Diamondback Rattlesnake. *Nat. Hist. Misc. Chicago Acad. Sci.* (34):1-3.

Landreth, H.F. 1973. Orientation and behavior of the rattlesnake, *Crotalus atrox. Copeia* 1973(1):26-31.

Minton, S.A. and S.A. Weinstein. 1986. Geographic and ontogenetic variation in venom of the Western Diamondback Rattlesnake *(Crotalus atrox). Toxicon* 24(1):71-80.

Perez, J.C., W.C. Haws, V.E. Garcia, and B.M. Jennings, III. 1978. Resistance of warm-blooded animals to snake venoms. *Toxicon* 16(4):375-383.

Price, A.H. 1988. Observations on maternal behavior and neonate aggregation in the Western Diamondback Rattlesnake, *Crotalus atrox* (Crotalidae). *Southwest. Nat.* 33(3):370-373.

Price, A.H. and J.L. LaPointe. 1990. Activity patterns of a Chihuahuan Desert snake community. *Ann. Carnegie Mus.* 59(1):15-23.

Straight, R., J.L. Glenn, and C.C. Snyder. 1976. Antivenom activity of rattlesnake blood plasma. *Nature* 261:259-260.

Tinkle, D.W. 1962. Reproductive potential and cycles in female *Crotalus atrox* from northwestern Texas. *Copeia* 1962(2):306-313.

Timber Rattlesnake:

Brown, C.W. and C.H. Ernst. 1986. A study of variation in eastern Timber Rattlesnakes, *Crotalus horridus* Linnae (Serpentes: Viperidae). *Brimleyana* (12):57-74.

Brown, W.S. 1991. Female reproductive ecology in a northern population of the Timber Rattlesnake, *Crotalus horridus. Herpetologica* 47(1):101-115.

Brown, W.S. 1993. Biology, status, and management of the Timber Rattlesnake *(Crotalus horridus)*: a guide for conservation. *SSAR Herpetol. Circ.* (22):vi + 78 p.

Fitch, H.S. 1985. Observations on rattle size and demography of Prairie Rattlesnakes *(Crotalus viridis)* and Timber Rattlesnakes *(Crotalus horridus)* in Kansas. *Occ. Pap. Mus. Nat. Hist. Univ. Kansas* (118):1-11.

Gibbons, J.W. 1972. Reproduction, growth, and sexual dimorphism in the Canebrake Rattlesnake *(Crotalus horridus atricaudatus). Copeia* 1972(2):222-226.

Glenn, J.L., R.C. Straight, and T.B. Wolt. 1994. Regional variation in the presence of Canebrake toxin in *Crotalus horridus* venom. *Comp. Biochem. Physiol.* 107C(3):337-346.

Kennedy, J.P. 1964. Natural history notes on some snakes of eastern Texas. *Texas J. Sci.* 16(2):210-215.

Pisani, G.R., J.T. Collins, and S.R. Edwards. 1972[1973]. A re-evaluation of the subspecies of *Crotalus horridus. Trans. Kansas Acad. Sci.*

75(3):255-263.

Reinert, H.K., D. Cundall, and L.M. Bushar. 1984. Foraging behavior of the Timber Rattlesnake, *Crotalus horridus*. *Copeia* 1984(4):976-981.

Reinert, H.K. and R.T. Zappalorti. 1988. Timber Rattlesnakes *(Crotalus horridus)* of the Pine Barrens: their movement patterns and habitat preference. *Copeia* 1988(4):964-978.

Rudolph, D.C. and S.J. Burgdorf. 1997. Timber Rattlesnakes and Louisiana Pine Snakes of the West Gulf Coastal Plain: hypotheses of decline. *Texas J. Sci.* 49(3)Suppl.:111-122.

Rock Rattlesnake:

Beaupre, S.J. 1995. Comparative ecology of the Mottled Rock Rattlesnake, *Crotalus lepidus*, in Big Bend National Park. *Herpetologica* 51(1):45-56.

Beaupre, S.J. 1996. Field metabolic rate, water flux, and energy budgets of Mottled Rock Rattlesnakes, *Crotalus lepidus*, from two populations. *Copeia* 1996(2):319-329.

Forstner, M.R.J., R.A. Hilsenbeck, and J.F. Scudday. 1997. Geographic variation in whole venom profiles from the Mottled Rock Rattlesnake *(Crotalus lepidus lepidus)* in Texas. *J. Herpetol.* 31(2):277-287.

Jacob, J.S. and J.S. Altenbach. 1977. Sexual color dimorphism in *Crotalus lepidus klauberi* Gloyd (Reptilia, Serpentes, Viperidae). *J. Herpetol.* 11(1):81-84.

Vincent, J.W. 1982. Phenotypic variation in *Crotalus lepidus lepidus* (Kennicott). *J. Herpetol.* 16(2):189-191.

Vincent, J.W. 1982. Color pattern variation in *Crotalus lepidus lepidus* (Viperidae) in southwestern Texas. *Southwest. Nat.* 27(3):263-272.

Blacktail Rattlesnake:

Beaupre, S.J. 1993. An ecological study of oxygen consumption in the Mottled Rock Rattlesnake, *Crotalus lepidus lepidus,* and the Black-Tailed Rattlesnake, *Crotalus molossus molossus,* from two populations. *Physiol. Zool.* 66(3):437-454.

Beck, D.D. 1995. Ecology and energetics of three sympatric rattlesnake species in the Sonoran Desert. *J. Herpetol.* 29(2):211-223.

Beck, D.D. 1996. Effects of feeding on body temperatures of rattlesnakes: a field experiment. *Physiol. Zool.* 69(6):1442-1455.

Dunkle, D.H. and H.M. Smith. 1937. Notes on some Mexican ophidians. *Occ. Pap. Mus. Zool. Univ. Michigan* (363):1-15.

Greene, H.W. 1994. Systematics and natural history, foundations for understanding and conserving biodiversity. *Amer. Zool.* 34(1):48-56.

Price, A.H. 1980. *Crotalus molossus. Cat. Amer. Amphib. Rept.*:242.1-242.2.

Rael, E.D., J.Z. Rivas, T. Chen, N. Maddux, E. Huizar, and C.S. Lieb. 1997. Differences in fibrinolysis and complement inactivation by venom from different Northern Blacktailed Rattlesnakes *(Crotalus molossus molossus)*. *Toxicon* 35(4):505-513.

Mojave Rattlesnake:

Glenn, J.L., R.C. Straight, M.C. Wolfe, and D.L. Hardy. 1983. Geographical variation in *Crotalus scutulatus scutulatus* (Mojave Rattlesnake) venom properties. *Toxicon* 21(1):119-130.

Hardy, D.L. 1983. Envenomation by the Mojave Rattlesnake *(Crotalus scutulatus scutulatus)* in southern Arizona, U.S.A. *Toxicon* 21(1):111-118.

Jacob, J.S. 1977. An evaluation of the possibility of hybridization between the rattlesnakes *Crotalus atrox* and *C. scutulatus* in the southwestern United States. *Southwest. Nat.* 22(4):469-485.

Jacob, J.S., S.R. Williams, and R.P. Reynolds. 1987. Reproductive activity of male *Crotalus atrox* and *C. scutulatus* (Reptilia: Viperidae) in northeastern Chihuahua, Mexico. *Southwest. Nat.* 32(2):273-276.

Mendelson, J.R., III and W.B. Jennings. 1992. Shifts in the relative abundance of snakes in a desert grassland. *J. Herpetol.* 26(1):38-45.

Price, A.H. 1982. *Crotalus scutulatus. Cat. Amer. Amphib. Rept.*:291.1-291.2.

Reynolds, R.P. and N.J. Scott, Jr. 1982. Use of a mammalian resource by a Chihuahuan snake community, p. 99-118. *In* N.J. Scott, Jr. (ed.), *Herpetological Communities*, U.S. Dept. Interior, Fish Wildl. Serv., Wildl. Res. Rep. (13): iv + 239 p.

Smith, H.M. 1990. Signs and symptoms following human envenomation by the Mojave Rattlesnake, *Crotalus scutulatus*, treated without use of antivenom. *Bull. Maryland Herpetol. Soc.* 26(3):105-110.

Wilkinson, J.A., J.L. Glenn, R.C. Straight, and J.W. Sites, Jr. 1991. Distribution and genetic variation in venom A and B populations of the Mojave Rattlesnake *(Crotalus scutulatus scutulatus)* in Arizona. *Herpetologica* 47(1):54-68.

Zepeda, H., E.D. Rael, and R.A. Knight. 1985. Isolation of two phospholipases A_2 from Mojave Rattlesnake *(Crotalus scutulatus scutulatus)* venom and variation of immunologically related venom properties in different populations. *Comp. Biochem. Physiol.* 81B(2):319-324.

Western Rattlesnake:

Aldridge, R.D. 1993. Male reproductive anatomy and seasonal occurrence of mating and combat behavior of the rattlesnake *Crotalus v. viridis. J. Herpetol.* 27(4):481-484.

Duvall, D., D. Chiszar, W.K. Hayes, J.K. Leonhardt, and M.J. Goode. 1990. Chemical and behavioral ecology of foraging in prairie rattlesnakes *(Crotalus viridis viridis). J. Chem. Ecol.* 16(1):87-101.

Duvall, D., M.J. Goode, W.K. Hayes, J.K. Leonhardt, and D.G. Brown. 1990. Prairie Rattlesnake vernal migration: field experimental analyses and survival value. *Natl. Geogr. Res.* 6(4):457-469.

Duvall, D., M.B. King, and K.J. Gutzwiller. 1985. Behavioral ecology and ethology of the Prairie Rattlesnake. *Natl. Geogr. Res.* 1(1):80-111.

Fiero, M.K., M.W. Seifert, T.J. Weaver, and C.A. Bonilla.1972. Comparative study of juvenile and adult Prairie Rattlesnake *(Crotalus viridis viridis)* venoms. *Toxicon* 10(1):81-82.

Furry, K., T. Swain, and D. Chiszar. 1991. Strike-induced chemosensory searching and trail following by Prairie Rattlesnakes *(Crotalus viridis)* preying upon deer mice *(Peromyscus maniculatus)*: chemical discrimination among individual mice. *Herpetologica* 47(1):69-78.

Graves, B.M. and D. Duvall. 1993. Reproduction, rookery use, and thermoregulation in free-ranging, pregnant *Crotalus v. viridis. J. Herpetol.* 27(1):33-41.

Graves, B.M., D. Duvall, M.B. King, S.L. Lindstedt, and W.A. Gern. 1986. Initial den location by neonatal prairie rattlesnakes: functions, causes, and natural history in chemical ecology, p. 285-304. *In* D. Duvall, D. Mueller-Schwarze, and R.M. Silverstein (eds.), *Chemical Signals in Vertebrates 4: Ecology, Evolution, and Comparative Biology.* Plenum Press, New York.

Jacob, J.S. and C.W. Painter. 1980. Overwinter thermal ecology of *Crotalus viridis* in the north-central plains of New Mexico. *Copeia* 1980(4):799-805.

King, M.B. and D. Duvall. 1990. Prairie Rattlesnake seasonal migrations: episodes of movement, vernal foraging and sex differences. *Anim. Behav.* 39(5):924-935.

Massasauga:

Chiszar, D., K. Scudder, H.M. Smith, and C.W. Radcliffe. 1976. Observation of courtship behavior in the Western Massasauga *(Sistrurus catenatus tergeminus). Herpetologica* 32(3):337-338.

Greene, H.W. and G.V. Oliver, Jr. 1965. Notes on the natural history of the Western Massasauga. *Herpetologica* 21(3):225-228.

Knopf, G.N. and D.W. Tinkle. 1961. The distribution and habits of *Sistrurus catenatus* in northwest Texas. *Herpetologica* 17(2):126-131.

Prior, K.A. and P.J. Weatherhead. 1994. Response of free-ranging Eastern Massasauga Rattlesnakes to human disturbance. *J. Herpetol.* 28(2):255-257.

Reinert, H.K. and W.R. Kodrich. 1982. Movements and habitat utilization by the Massasauga, *Sistrurus catenatus catenatus*. *J. Herpetol.* 16(2):162-171.

Seigel, R.A. 1986. Ecology and conservation of an endangered rattlesnake, *Sistrurus catenatus*, in Missouri, USA. *Biol. Conserv.* 35(4):333-346.

Weatherhead, P.J. and K.A. Prior. 1992. Preliminary observations of habitat use and movements of the Eastern Massasauga Rattlesnake (*Sistrurus c. catenatus*). *J. Herpetol.* 26(4):447-452.

Pygmy Rattlesnake:

Bishop, L.A., T.M. Farrell, and P.G. May. 1996. Sexual dimorphism in a Florida population of the rattlesnake *Sistrurus miliarius*. *Herpetologica* 52(3):360-364.

Carpenter, C.C. 1960. A large brood of Western Pigmy Rattlesnakes. *Herpetologica* 16(1):142-143.

Farrell, T.M., P.G. May, and M.A. Pilgrim. 1995. Reproduction in the rattlesnake, *Sistrurus miliarius barbouri*, in central Florida. *J. Herpetol.* 29(1):21-27.

Ford, N.B., V.A. Cobb, and W.W. Lamar. 1990. Reproductive data on snakes from northeastern Texas. *Texas J. Sci.* 42(4):355-368.

Marchisin, A. 1978. Observations on an audio-visual "warning" signal in the Pigmy Rattlesnake, *Sistrurus miliarius* (Reptilia, Serpentes, Crotalidae). *Herpetol. Rev.* 9(3):92-93.

May, P.G., T.M. Farrell, S.T. Heulett, M.A. Pilgrim, L.A. Bishop, D.J. Spence, A.M. Rabatsky, M.G. Campbell, A.D. Aycrigg, and W.E. Richardson II. 1996. Seasonal abundance and activity of a rattlesnake (*Sistrurus miliarius barbouri*) in central Florida. *Copeia* 1996(2):389-401.

Rabatsky, A.M and T.M. Farrell. 1996. The effects of age and light level on foraging posture and frequency of caudal luring in the rattlesnake, *Sistrurus miliarius barbouri*. *J. Herpetol.* 30(4):558-561.

Harlequin Coral Snake:

Beckers, G.J.L., T.A.A.M. Leenders, and H. Strijbosch. 1996. Coral snake mimicry: live snakes not avoided by a mammalian predator. *Oecologia*

106(4):461-463.

Brodie, E.D., III and F.J. Janzen. 1995. Experimental studies of coral snake mimicry: generalized avoidance of ringed snake patterns by free-ranging avian predators. *Funct.Ecol.* 9(2):186-190.

Fix, J.D. and S.A. Minton, Jr. 1976. Venom extraction and yields from the North American coral snake, *Micrurus fulvius. Toxicon* 14(2):143-145.

Greene, H.W. 1984. Feeding behavior and diet of the Eastern Coral Snake, *Micrurus fulvius. Univ. Kansas Mus. Nat. Hist. Spec. Publ.* (10):147-162

Greene, H.W. and R.W. McDiarmid. 1981. Coral snake mimicry: does it occur? *Science* 213:1207-1212.

Jackson, D.R. and R. Franz. 1981. Ecology of the Eastern Coral Snake *(Micrurus fulvius)* in northern peninsular Florida. *Herpetologica* 37(4):213-228.

Kennedy, J.P. 1964. Natural history notes on some snakes of eastern Texas. *Texas J. Sci.* 16(2):210-215.

Kitchens, C.S. and L.H.S. Van Mierop. 1987. Envenomation by the Eastern Coral Snake *(Micrurus fulvius fulvius)*: a study of 39 victims. *J. Amer. Med. Assoc.* 258(12):1615-1618.

Peterson, K.H. 1990. Conspecific and self-envenomation in snakes. *Bull. Chicago Herpetol. Soc.* 25:26-28.

Quinn, H.R. 1979. Reproduction and growth of the Texas Coral Snake *(Micrurus fulvius tenere)*. *Copeia* 1979(3):453-463.

Roze, J.A. 1996. *Coral Snakes of the Americas: Biology, Identification, and Venoms*. Krieger Publ. Co., Malabar, Florida. xii + 328 p.